Straight Shooting

pastoral reflections

for today's church

by
William F. Harrell

Foreword by Dr. Paige Patterson

ISBN 978-0-9826561-5-0

Printed in the United States of America by
Lightning Source, Inc.

Cover Design by Debbie Patrick, www.visionrun.com

Unless otherwise indicated, all Scripture taken from the King James Version of the Holy Bible

Free Church Press
P.O. Box 1075
Carrollton, GA 30112

Content

"Wise words from the head and heart of one of Southern Baptists' most effective pastors."

—Jerry Vines

"Bill Harrell has been the effective pastor of the wonderful Abilene Baptist Church in Augusta for more than 30 years, but he has never been known to mince words. He calls a spade a spade or in his book "Straight Shooting" *Harrell calls a camel a camel and sugar coats zilch. If you are looking for a book that reflects the honest, unvarnished observations of a pastor about today's national crisis, denominational decline and troubled church you need look no further. Harrell's descriptive artistry is not depicted in pale pastels, but in brilliant colors so there is no doubt as to the impression he desires to make upon the reader. Not everyone will agree with his conclusions, but everyone will know that Harrell is a man of convictions and passion."*

—Gerald Harris, Editor, The Christian Index

"Straight Shooting *is nothing new for Bill Harrell. He's been shooting straight for as long as I've known him. I've never had to wonder where Bill Harrell stood on an issue! You may find his "practical reflections" personally challenging, but they will certainly make you think! Thank you Bill for not only being a "straight shooter," but for being consistent throughout your ministry!*

—Ernest Easley, Senior Pastor of Roswell Street Baptist Church, Marietta, GA

In his new book, Straight Shooting, *Bill Harrell takes aim, fires and hits the bull's-eye! He is dead center with his warnings about the moral decadence of this nation and the struggle of the church of our Lord Jesus Christ in this postmodern era. Dr. Harrell's questions and observations are razor sharp, just as God's Word is the two-edged sword of the Lord.* Straight Shooting *is written with conviction, clarity and brevity; easily read by pastors and laymen alike who have been praying for a powerful spiritual awakening to sweep this country. The words within will penetrate your soul and challenge your heart!*

—Morris Chapman, Former President and Chief Executive Officer, SBC Executive Committee

The Abilene Baptist Church

in

Martinez, Georgia

lovingly dedicates this volume to our

beloved Pastor of over thirty-one years

The Rev. William F. Harrell

affectionately known by our church family as

"Brother Bill"

for his courageous leadership...

for his intellectual depth...

for his listening ear...

for his servant's heart...

for his prophetic voice...

for his powerful preaching...

and for his godly wife, Carolyn.

We thank our Heavenly Father

that He chose to send to us

Brother Bill

"for such a time as this"

(Esther 4:14)

Foreword

Do not touch *Straight Shooting: Pastoral Reflections for Today's Church* by William F. Harrell if you are just looking for something to read as sleep inducement at bed time. Leave it strictly alone if you are charmed by the politically correct. If your motivation in life is to be at ease in Zion, put this little monograph down now— no, throw it out the window; no, run to the closest ocean and toss it lest someone discovers it and is awakened from the slumber of post-modernity.

As the subtitle indicates, these perspectives are the product of a long, fruitful pastoral journey from the mind of one of the most colorful pastors of our era. The reader will experience amusement, enlightenment, acquiescence, fury, glee, tears, sorrow, and joy—all in the short space of this entertaining and thought-provoking pilgrimage. Even if this little monograph irritates you, you should be warned that to initiate the reading of these thoughts is to set the hook in your own jaws!

If there exist somewhere politicians, civil servants, ecclesiastical leaders, or educators who care to know how the average American is thinking or become acquainted with the questions throbbing in his mind, a quick read of Pastor Harrell's *Straight Shooting* might prove to be the most salubrious vacation that he could take. You may or may not agree, but you will do some profitable thinking.

As a supporter of the second amendment to the U.S. Constitution, I have always believed that the right of Americans to bear arms needs to be accentuated by the ability to shoot straight. Shooting straight, after all, is about the only way to hit something significant. As an ardent advocate of gun control, defined as "steady aim," the entire social order is in need of more leaders like Pastor Bill Harrell, who, as he demonstrates in this book, is more concerned with telling the truth than with being popular. No place for wimps here—read at your own risk—and delight.

Paige Patterson

President

Southwestern Baptist Theological Seminary

Fort Worth, Texas

Chapter 1

Forum on the Separation of Church and State

I think it would be befitting at the outset of this discussion to talk about what the separation of church and state actually is and what it means in reality. First, where did the statement originate? In our society the populace has been educated to believe that the separation of church and state is a doctrine which was carefully crafted by the founding fathers to make sure that the church and the religious community should have no say whatsoever in anything which even remotely touches the political spectrum. They believe that the phrase "separation of church and state" is a legitimate doctrine which is contained in our founding documents when in actuality it is not. One can search until the proverbial "cows come home," and they will not find that phrase or any such doctrine in our Constitution. Just for the record, the First Amendment states: "Congress shall make no law respecting an establishment of religion; or prohibiting the free exercise thereof; or abridging the freedom of speech, or the press; or the right of the people peaceably to assemble, and to petition the government for a redress of grievances." No mention is made of a "wall between church and state." So, where did the phrase "separation of church and state" originate?

In 1802, Thomas Jefferson received a letter from the Danbury Baptist Association in Connecticut which was very concerned

9

about the fact that the government might affect the free expression of their faith by formally establishing a state church. Thomas Jefferson was sympathetic with their concerns and within the body of his letter answering them, he reassured them that they would not be restricted in the free expression of their faith by employing the metaphor "wall of separation between church and state." His actual quote is: "I contemplate with sovereign reverence that act of the whole American people which declared that their legislature should make no law respecting an establishment of religion, or prohibiting the free exercise thereof, thus building a wall of separation between Church and State." It should be noted that what Jefferson was writing in reference to was the fact that the Danbury Baptist Association should have no fear of the "national" government imposing a religion on a state. He saw that as a states' rights issue. Jefferson's letter had nothing to say about limiting public religious expression but dealt with government's interference in the public expression of faith. Interestingly, Jefferson allowed, and even attended, church services in the U.S. Capitol, the Treasury and the War Department buildings, and the Supreme Court. In fact, he wrote his letter to the Danbury Baptists on Friday, and two days later he rode his horse to the Capitol Building and attended church services in the Capitol Building with about 2,000 other people. Now, I ask you, does that sound like someone who was concerned about the government's participation in the expression of religious faith as some would say? I think not!

So, the expression "wall of separation between church and state" was a part of a private letter from Thomas Jefferson to the Danbury Baptist Association. In his letter it is nothing more than a metaphor, a figure of speech, but it has now been inculcated into our society in such a way that it literally means that secular society must be sanitized from the presence of religious influence. It might also be valuable to remember the situation our forefathers were recalling when the fear of a state church became a question for them. They had just come from England where there was a state church, The Church of England. They had to worship under the aegis of that church or else suffer the consequences, and they did not want that to happen over here in the new country.

Just as an example, the original pastor of Abilene Baptist Church was a man named Loveless Savage. He had been the High Sheriff for the British Crown in this part of the world. A preacher named Daniel Marshall came into the area preaching that a person should be baptized only after conversion. This was against the Church of England's practice, and so it was considered against the law to preach it even though the Bible affirms what Marshall was preaching. Daniel Marshall, the preacher was arrested by Loveless Savage, the sheriff, for preaching against the Church of England's teachings. A short time later Savage was converted; and God called him to preach. Marshall ordained him and then formed Abilene Baptist Church with the old sheriff as the first pastor. The point being that there was persecution from a state church in those days, and the people wanted to be free from that. That is why the first amendment states that "Congress shall make no law respecting an establishment of religion; or prohibiting the free exercise thereof."

Secondly, what is the effect of our secular application of the phrase, "separation of church and state?" The ACLU and the Americans United for the Separation of Church and State use this Jeffersonian metaphor as a tool in an attempt to separate religion from the public square. The most cherished freedom we have as Americans is our freedom of speech. Everyone has the right to express themselves openly – except the church, and because of their position, the pastors in particular. The one place that we should want to be completely free is the very one that is limited by governmental influence. So, everyone can say what they want, when they want to say it. Everyone, that is, except the church. Everyone can publicly express their opinions. Everyone, that is, except the church.

The secular world, does not want to hear from God on the issues of the day. It does not want God's appointed prophets to have influence in its realm. So, how do you limit them? A very shrewd politician found the answer in 1954, and his name was Lyndon Johnson. While running for the senate, Mr. Johnson was being called into question by a leading Texas evangelist. This evangelist was giving the senator a hard time and was beginning to have strong influence on the voters. So, Mr. Johnson simply had his friends in the system to incorporate a ruling in the tax code which stated that churches and religious organizations could not enter into the political arena as long as they received consideration from the IRS and did not have to pay taxes. If they violated the ruling, then the IRS would investigate them and fine them for their offense as well as revoke their tax exempt status.

So, let's think for a moment about what this ruling really implies. It says that of all people in America, only the preachers and the churches have a point at which they are not totally free, and that is at our most cherished point: the freedom of speech. It is also, in effect, holding the churches and preachers hostage at the price of whatever their taxes would be if they paid taxes. If we speak certain things and if the church does certain things, we will lose our tax exempt 501(c)(3) status. The one place that should be kept free, our pulpits, is held hostage for the price of tax monies. This should not be.

I would also like to ask this question: Does this mean then, that if a church decided to voluntarily surrender its 501(c)(3) status, that it could enter the political arena? Churches in Georgia already pay state sales tax so just suppose that a church said: "Ok, we voluntarily agree to pay all taxes." Would that set them free? If the price of tax monies is holding them hostage, then it follows that if that is , they would be free from the current restrictions. The only difference it would really make is that the church would have to pay property taxes (it already pays state sales tax in Ga.), and the people would lose a tax deduction. If a church voluntarily surrendered its 501(c)(3) status and therefore paid the appropriate taxes, it would then be free to enter into the political arena and say whatever it desires. If that is true, then it is proven that the, so called, separation of church and state is NOT a constitutional issue. If it were a constitutional issue then whether a church paid taxes or not would make no difference. If a church is set free from the applied restraints by paying taxes, then it is demonstrated that the constitution is not the governing force, but the IRS is.

Incidentally, prior to 1953, churches and their pastors were not restricted. That is why the aforementioned evangelist could speak out on Lyndon Johnson's senate race as he did. Since that IRS ruling, religion in the public square has been restricted to the point of almost total exclusion, and if the ACLU and The Americans United for the Separation of Church and State had their way that is exactly what would happen. The church and its followers should not be quarantined or walled off from where civic discourse takes place.

The restrictions on religion have reached the point of absurdity such as: threatening fixed income housing project residents with eviction for displaying signs about prayer in their apartment windows; prohibiting students from praying at graduation ceremonies or football games; having public displays of the Ten commandments removed from public buildings; telling an eight year old girl that she cannot pass out handmade Valentines that read "Jesus Loves You"; making pupils who have on a t-shirt with anything remotely religious inscribed on them to go home and change; telling employees that they cannot wear a piece of jewelry to work if it is in the shape of a cross. I could go on and on, but you would get bored with the absurdities of how the Jeffersonian metaphor has been extrapolated into our society.

But, I think the tide is turning. Recently, the U.S. Court of Appeals for the 6th Circuit, expressed its frustration over the misuse of Jefferson's metaphor. Ruling on the constitutionality of a Ten Commandments display in Kentucky, the court wrote, "This extra-constitutional construct has grown tiresome. The First Amendment does not demand a wall of separation between church and state." They are right! It does not. Additionally, the tide is also turning in dealing with liberal groups such as the ACLU and the Americans United for the Separation of Church and State. Of course, the mainstream media reports to the nation every time the ACLU wins a court case or when they extort obeisance from a small county or town by threatening them with a multimillion dollar lawsuit unless they do whatever it is the ACLU demands. But, the media has been strangely silent on how many cases the ACLU is now losing because of defeats in the courtroom as they have faced informed lawyers from organizations such as The Alliance Defense Fund. They are losing case after case, but the public will never know it because a liberal media base will not tell them about it. Also, the ruling by the U.S. Court of Appeals for the 6th Circuit signals that the courts are tiring of the ACLU's endless appeals to the First Amendment for the basis of their endless, insipid lawsuits. The American public must be wise enough to see that the ACLU and such groups would go out of business if the First Amendment and their appeal to the supposed "separation of church and state" were taken from them. They have no other basis for their suits.

Finally, I would hope that a day is coming in which this nation will demand the proper interpretation of the First Amendment. I would hope that we could return to the common sense approach of our founding fathers when they provided that our federal government could not tell people which faith they should follow while, at the same time, making room for the public discourse to contain input from the religious community. Again, I want to thank the organizers of this forum for being so gracious in extending me an invitation to participate.

Chapter 2

The Death of Death

I have just been reading an article in the *Chronicle of Higher Education* dealing with the possibility that people could live a thousand years or even longer if the findings and research of Aubrey de Gray prove true. He is an English bio-gerontologist who is making some profound observations concerning our ability to live longer. He is, of course, talking about using medical procedures of various kinds to reverse some of the things which cause aging. He is also talking about growing new organs in the lab from stem cells in order to replace worn out ones. He is being heralded as the man who will "murder" death.

I don't want to throw water on Mr. de Gray's fire, but it just won't happen. God has said long ago that "it is appointed unto man once to die, but after this, the judgment."...Hebrews 9:27. Mr. de Gray is simply trying to do something that is impossible because he is trying to solve a spiritual problem with medical and "mechanical" means. He is attempting to do what humans have been trying for thousands of years to do, and that is to get back into the "garden of Eden" without a relationship with God. All of human history attests to this desire. Once Adam and Eve were put out of the garden because of sin, they have been struggling to find a way to get back in. Immortality was one of the things humans experienced in Eden. Adam and Eve were created to live forever and have an unending and blissful relationship with God day to day. Mr. de Gray is trying to restore the eternal life characteristic to human beings without so much as dealing with the spiritual nature of the problem we now face with death.

Initially, humans lived longer than they do now. Biblical characters prove humans lived longer. Methuselah lived for 969 years. Enoch lived 365 years. Lamech, the father of Noah, lived 777 years. Noah himself, lived 950 years. The longer man has been on the earth, the shorter the time he has lived. Why is this true? The reason is found in the fact that man's perfect genetic code which allowed unending life was corrupted by this thing God calls sin. The longer humans have lived on earth, the more the code has been corrupted resulting in a decrease in the life span humans naturally experience. Death is not a natural state for man as far as God is concerned. He "engineered" man to live forever with Him in the Garden of Eden. But man corrupted himself with sin, and death entered the world.

In these modern days we have been able to increase the human life span somewhat, but it has not been done because we have dealt properly with the root cause of death...sin. We have made living conditions better. We have invented medicines and procedures which help us live longer. We have found better ways to eat and exercise. In general we have improved our lives greatly. But remember this: *death is still universal.* Everyone dies physically eventually. Mr. de Gray can postulate all he desires, but he is not going to solve the problem of physical death.

And then, I have posed this question to a lot of people: Would you like to live to be say...300 years old? You might be surprised to learn that even though people in general fear death, I have not found a single person who answers "yes" to that question. Nearly universally, they say that they would tire of life at extreme ages. They can't imagine dealing with the growing problems in the world which surely will get worse. The thought of outliving everyone they know is depressing to them. Most people say that they want to live a normal lifetime and then die peacefully.

But, you see, Mr. de Gray is trying to solve a problem the world almost universally wants to reject, and that is the problem of judgment. He surmises that if people could live forever they would never have to face judgment. But, judgment is no problem to those who *will* live forever, and those are the people who have trusted in God's way of solving the problem of death and separation. Those are the ones who have eternal life given to them as a gift when they trust their lives to Jesus Christ, God's only way of solving our sin and death problem.

So, Mr. de Gray and all others who might hold to his views are coming at the problem of death and eternal life from the wrong direction. They want life to continue by solving the medical and physical side of aging. They should be looking at it from the other perspective and that is this: The solution to death is to be found when one comes at the issue from God's perspective, and that perspective is focused on the person of Jesus Christ who gives us the eternal life man so readily gave up when Adam and Eve sinned in the Garden of Eden.

Want to live forever? You can when you go at it from God's pathway which leads to eternal life through Jesus Christ. And, by the way…the Death of Death has already taken place. It happened when Jesus Christ was raised from the dead, thereby defeating death and making eternal life possible for anyone who will come to God by Him.

Chapter 3

No Fear of the Inconceivable

It is a fact that a person will not fear that which he or she cannot conceive. In the Biblical days the people who were drowned in the flood were warned repeatedly, but they failed to listen. The reason was that they could not conceive of what Noah was telling them about an impending flood that would cover the face of the earth and kill every living thing. It was beyond their ability to understand, so they had no fear of it at all. They watched Noah build the ark for 120 years and never took his warnings. It was inconceivable to them that such a thing would happen.

We have a situation today which is inconceivable to the human mind, and therefore our legislators and the public are unafraid of it. I am referencing the situation we have with our national debt. We hear a lot about the annual deficit and we have become used to talking about two or three hundred billion dollars as if that in itself is understandable. Recently our government loaned huge sums of money to companies and institutions in order to keep them from collapsing in the credit fiasco. But what about those sums of money? How can the public possibly know the magnitude of the sums of money being discussed? I have done some investigating and calculating, and I want to try to make it more understandable to the people who are paying the bill…the American taxpayer.

Consider this: A million dollars (which, by itself is larger than the average person can conceive) is represented by one thousand, $1,000 dollar bills (which are no longer printed). One million dollars is a stack of $1,000 dollar bills 4.75 inches high (measured in a local bank using one dollar bills which are the same thickness as a $ 1,000 dollar bill). One thousand times one thousand is one million. One billion dollars, and we speak of one billion as amounting to little or nothing in today's world, is one thousand times one million. So, that stack would be 1000 times 4.75 inches or 4750 inches divided by 12 which is 395.8 feet. So a billion dollars is a stack of $1000 dollar bills 395.8 feet straight up!

Now, let's carry it a little farther. One trillion dollars is equal to 1000 times one billion. Now how high is that stack? This is where it really gets scary. One trillion dollars is a stack of $1,000 dollar bills which is 74.9 miles high. This is calculated by taking the 395.8 feet of the one billion stack and multiplying it by 1,000. It turns out to be 395,800 feet which is divided by 5280 (one mile) and the result is 74.9 miles. So, a trillion dollars is a stack of $1,000 dollar bills 74.9 miles high. Our national debt is now about fourteen trillion dollars. That means that the stack of $1,000 dollar bills representing our current national debt is 1050 miles high. This also means that the astronauts in the space shuttle can look out the window (assuming that they are orbiting at about 250 miles), and it is approximately 800 more miles to the tip of the stack. Now, folks we are talking about a stack of $1,000 dollar bills!

Recently our government led us into a $700 billion dollar bailout (actually it was much more than this, but let's just use this figure.) If you do the calculations you will find that they are asking the American taxpayer to come up with a stack of $1,000 dollar bills 52.4 miles high in order to solve the financial crisis. Now that's a BIG crisis! Every billion dollars they discuss is a stack of $1,000 bills 395.8 feet high. You do the math. It will soon dawn on you that those people in Washington are dealing with numbers they cannot conceive, so that is why they have no fear of the magnitude of the financial decisions they are making.

One other little example: If each dollar of the 700 billion dollar bailout was represented by one second, how long a period of time would that be? And, if you were going to pay it off at one dollar a second, (with no new interest added) how far back in history would it transport you? In other words, how long is 700 billion seconds? It is 11,666,666,666.6 minutes or 194,444,444.4 hours or 8,101,851 days which being divided by 365 days gives you 22,196.85 years back into history. This is long before history was recorded. Friends, one trillion dollars would take approximately 32,000 years to pay off at one dollar a second. Now remember our national debt is about 14 trillion so it would take 448,000 years to pay it off at one dollar a second interest free! Staggering isn't it?

Now, you know why our Congress has no fear of what they are asking our country to do. They can't possibly conceive of the magnitude of what they are discussing. I think it is time they face the realities of what they are dealing with and get some semblance of common sense about what they are doing with our money because, as I stated earlier, there is No Fear of the Inconceivable, and because that is true, the door is opened for even greater problems to arise.

Chapter 4

Yup, It's A Camel!

It has often been said that a camel is really a fine, high bred, Tennessee walking horse which was designed by a Southern Baptist committee. People tend to start out with good intentions and ideas, but before a committee is finished with the task, it will somehow, and in some way, find a way to completely mess things up. The problem stems from the fact that everyone on the committee feels that they must contribute something to the deliberations or else they were non-functional in the whole process. There is also the old ego thing going on. Most committee members are not willing to submit to the suggestions and ideas of others without feeling that they too must be heard, and if their suggestions are not included in the solution, then their ego is bruised in some devastating way.

This situation is what the American people are presently facing with the Congress of the United States. Everyone there thinks that they just have to be heard and that they must prove their presence and worth by writing some outlandish piece of legislation or else by being the loudest spokesperson on a committee. Our Congress is producing a lot of camels these days. Sadly, the same model is followed in various states with their own state legislatures. They deal with somewhat smaller issues overall, but they still operate on the committee principles which have devastated lawmaking on the national level.

One has to wonder how in the world a group of senators and representatives whether national or state, can take some of the common sense issues of the day and turn them into a "camel." A few examples will help us understand this somewhat better. Take for instance, the issue of same sex marriage. Now, this is a no-brainer for common sense people. Everyone with a grain of intelligence can figure out that marriage is supposed to be between one man and one woman. God designed it that way and anything God has designed just can't be improved upon. But, it seems that on this one, the Federal Government has had a lot more sense than the state governments have had. It has largely stayed out of this argument, and I pray that they will remain on the sidelines permanently because if one thinks the states have confused the issue, then just wait until the Federal government gets through with it.

The real demon is political correctness. Just don't hurt anyone's feelings by telling them that what they are doing is wrong. Design a way to make them feel good about themselves. Redefine the family so that any group of nitwits living under a particular roof can expect that they will be treated the same as a legitimate family would be treated. Then when people with one modicum of common sense and decency look at the resulting group of people that society has defined as a family, they will be able to say…"Yup, It's a Camel!" Write laws to make it legal for unmarried people to have all the benefits of marriage as far as society is concerned. And as for marriage make sure that the committee approach has its day with it as well. Get some judges to declare what society will be like in spite of what the people say. Find some apostate minister or some idiot judge who will actually unite two men or two women in matrimony. Make sure they wear white for the purity of their union, and don't forget the kiss to seal the vows followed by a full reception at which a multitude of secular minded people will sip champagne and congratulate the new "couple." In other words, take something as simple and common sense as marriage and when the committees get through with it, you will find a monster standing in front of you. And, you will be saying..."Yup, It's a Camel!"

One of the best examples of how Washington can confuse and convolute and issue is Medicare. This was supposed to be a way to provide medical help to people who were not as fortunate financially as others. It was also supposed to benefit people who had reached 65 years of age. So, the "fine Tennessee walking horse" was to be something which would be a benefit to millions of people providing for them the possibility of medical coverage. As it turns out, after the work of Congress, it is of little benefit at all. One has to buy a supplement to go along with the Medicare which will cover what the program no longer covers if it ever did. All in all, one pays about as much as they would have paid for a private health policy after they pay for the Medicare coverage and then the supplemental insurance. All that has happened is that the Federal Government has gotten their fingers into that vast resource of funds which is expended in the medical field, and they are now in the process of messing it up so badly that we are going to have a shortage of doctors in only a few years because so many of them are getting out of the medical field due to the "Camel" the whole process has become. As we look at what was initially dreamed up...the fine Tennessee Walking horse, and compare it to what the Federal Government has turned it into, we would be correct in stating..."Yup, It's A Camel!"

And, Social Security...my, what a confused disaster it has become. Your Social Security money, and I say "your", was supposed to be kept safe by the government. In fact, you were promised that it would be protected. But, it has now been spent on other things to the point that Social Security will not be viable in only a few years. So, now the result of all this misuse of funds is that they have come up with the "sliding scale" of when a person is old enough to participate. This in an effort to make the funds last longer. But, at the same time our lawmakers have said that illegal aliens can tap into the resources. People who have nothing invested can get a check just like you do although they have put nothing into the system and are actually here illegally. So, someone has said: "I know what to do"…"let's fix it so we can tap into the private sector's retirement plans." "There are billions of dollars lying out there." "There is a sea of money just waiting to help us out on the Social Security crises." Friends, your IRA and other retirement vehicles are in danger. Watch out, they are designing another "Camel" and they want to use your private monies to do so.

The illegal immigration situation is a perfect example of what a "committee" of Senators and Representatives can design. "Let's let them come in." "We need the help with the work that Americans will no longer do." "Uh oh, too many are coming in." "Let's build a fence." "But, that isn't working, so let's put patrols on the fence" "But, let's keep it small." "Let's don't put troops there and do it right." "This thing is out of control." "We can't handle all of them coming here to work." "I know what! Let's just make all of them legal, and then we won't be faced with the problem of illegal aliens." Now, about that fence, common sense people declared that it would not work. The politicians were in need of doing something, anything at all, and a fence looked like a good idea to the Camel designers. Some fought the idea, but it's a high fence. And, wide too. But, it is full of gaps. It doesn't run the length of the border. Another example of "Camelizing." Then the same people who create the problem realize that there is something very valuable here. So, they arrange things so that these people who have nothing invested in America can vote and determine the future of this nation. Of course, they will vote for those who make it easy for them to be in the country without ever becoming a citizen in the prescribed, legal way. All in all, this thing with the illegal aliens is something of which one could exclaim…"Yup, It's A Camel!"

Not to be redundant, but an example we earlier considered makes this writer's point precisely. The $700 billion dollar bailout of the financial institutions as well as the billions of dollars to be spent on "bailing out" others as well such as the auto industry is a "camel" in the process of being created. Congress is in charge of discussing this and deciding what to do. After everyone adds his own little idea to the process, this too will become something that will not work. It won't be $700 billion dollars in the long run. It will be trillions of dollars spent to fix a system that is rotting away under the weight of corruption. It is absolutely insane for those who assured the Congress in sworn hearings that everything was all right with Fannie Mae and Freddie Mac to be sitting in on the committee, even chairing it, which is grilling those who are coming before them for help. Those individuals should be prosecuted for lying to the Congress and to the people. And, to top it all off, these men accepted huge sums of money from Fannie Mae and Freddie Mac. Something is terribly wrong here. Watch very carefully and you will observe as out-of-touch politicians put together something that common sense people will observe and mutter to themselves, "Yup, It's A Camel!"

Congress itself has become a Camel and it is doing what Camels do...breeding more Camels of like kind. In fact, if Congress were an individual, the collective intelligence and reasoning of Congress would qualify it to be put in an institution for the mentally deficient. It is time to turn the whole lot out to pasture and start all over again with some fine Tennessee Walking Horses.

Chapter 5

Faith and Choice

I suppose that there has never been an issue which divided our nation like the issue of abortion. Even though a majority of the people in our nation is presently against abortion, it continues to be the law of the land. Opinions concerning this medical procedure which terminates life range from those who are radically in favor of it to those who feel that it is nothing more than prescribed murder. Many citizens who say they are people of faith hold these same divergent views. So, the question is asked: How does one's faith impact his view of abortion? Some denominations actually state that they are in favor of choice while others are opposed to it. Different religions also hold opposing views concerning the termination of the life of the unborn child. Some feel that it should be a woman's choice as to whether to terminate a pregnancy or not, while others back up their pro-life position with Scripture.

This article is meant to help people be better informed so that they can make the proper decision concerning the issue of choice where abortion is concerned. And, one's faith does carry a tremendous amount of weight concerning where one stands. I would like to develop my approach in this paper not so much from an emotional position, but from a logical one. I think that good logic must be a vital part of the thinking process of those who are dealing with life and death. I also want it to be understood that as a pastor, I am in the Redemption Business. If I can help anyone who struggles with abortion, possibly having had one, I am more than willing to help them experience forgiveness and freedom from any guilt they might have associated with the procedure.

So, with that being said, think with me today about several things. It is necessary that we must go to the foundational issue at hand and that is human life and when it begins. There have been medical arguments for many years about the moment of life and when it begins. Now, since this forum is about faith and choice, I must go to the foundational document we have in order to draw some conclusions. Also, I would like to say that I have no negotiating room on this issue. I am bound by the Holy Scripture, the Bible which is unequivocal in its treatment of life. I have much more authority for my views than anyone holding a contrary view. Scripture is the final authority whether one wants to admit it or not. So, with that foundation, let me proceed.

First, from my source, the Scripture, I see that life begins at the moment of conception when sperm and egg come together, and the genetic materials in each of them are combined to form a human. God even tells us that He knows us before we are conceived. He knows your name before sperm and egg come together. In Jeremiah 1:5, this is recorded: "Before I formed thee in the womb, I knew thee; and before thou earnest forth out of the womb, I sanctified thee, and I ordained thee a prophet unto the nations." And in Isaiah 49:5, Isaiah said..." And now, saith the Lord who formed me from the womb to be his servant..."

Now someone may say, "I don't believe the Scripture." That is your prerogative. But think about this: if you are right and Scripture doesn't matter, then I have nothing to lose. But if I am right, and you are wrong; you have everything to lose. Logic. Also, every person in this room was once half egg and half sperm. Every person was once a zygote. The very reason you are here today is that you were left in your mother's womb. You were left alone, and you developed into who you are. It is very easy for people to be pro-choice from this perspective, but I would wager that if you had been given the option from the pre-birth perspective, you would have been pro-Life. Judgments are easy from this side. From the moment of conception, all the genetic material to product a unique individual is present. The chromosomes and genes begin to arrange themselves, and they determine everything about you. You had brown or blue eyes before you had eyes. You were tall before you grew up. You were going to be bald before the first hair fell out.

You are unique. King David says this about it: "I will praise thee; for I am fearfully and wonderfully made. Marvelous are thy works, and that my soul knoweth right well. My substance was not hidden from thee, when I was made in secret, and intricately wrought in the lowest parts of the earth. Thine eyes did see my substance, yet being unformed; and in thy book all my members were fashioned, when as yet there was none of them," Ps. 139:14-16.

Secondly, the law recognizes that human life begins with conception. Let me demonstrate. In both Georgia and South Carolina, in recent days and two separate events, a man was charged with vehicular homicide because he carelessly caused the death of another with his automobile. Both men were charged more than once even though only one person had been killed. They were charged with two deaths because the woman who was killed was pregnant and the child died also. Question: if the law did not legally recognize the human validity of that unborn life, then why was someone charged with the death of the unborn infant?

We have a serious lapse of logic here concerning abortion and whether it is murder or not. On the one hand we have a person who plans the death of another. He carefully decides how and when he will kill the person. When he is caught he is charged with first degree homicide for planning a murder and pulling it off. On the other hand we have someone who no less plans the death of a person (an unborn infant) and in the most sterile conditions goes through with the killing. But, they are paid for their services. Their logic runs into itself on this one. People are jailed all the time for paying money for someone to kill another person for them. The difference is that the Supreme Court has wrongly said that it is o.k. to destroy the life of a child in an abortion.

And yet, we speak of a woman's right to choose. Choose what? To end a life that even criminal law says one can be punished for destroying? God gives us a little lesson on this in Exodus 21:22-23, "…if men strive, and hurt a woman with child so that her fruit depart from her, and yet no mischief follows; he shall be surely punished, according as the woman's husband will lay upon him; and he shall pay as the judges determine. And if any mischief follows, then thou shalt give life for life." I think that pretty well sums it up. I want to make this observation for you: *The Supreme Court does not hold court in heaven.* I just wonder what a person will say when God confronts them with the fact that they performed abortions. I can just hear it now: "Well you see, God, our Supreme Court said it was acceptable to do that so makes it o.k. for us to do.'" I don't think God is going to accept that.

In fact, God tells us a foundational truth when He says: "Thou Shalt Not Kill." Any student of Hebrew or Greek will tell you that God was not talking here about defending one's self or their country. He was talking about the premeditated taking of a human life. We are not to do that. Additionally, one can do serious prison time for destroying the egg of a Bald eagle. Now, why? It is because the Bald eagle is an endangered species. Question: if that little bird in the egg is not already a Bald Eagle, then why would one be charged and jailed for destroying it? But yet, we perform abortions and try to tell people that it is not a human because it is not born yet? The sad thing is that we value a Bald Eagle chick more than we value human life in incubation in the womb.

Professor John Harris, a member of the British Medical Association's ethics committee said: ""It is not plausible to think that there is any moral change that occurs during the journey down the birth canal." He was suggesting that the moral status of the fetus and the human infant outside the womb should be seen as the same. He asserted, "There is no obvious reason why one should think differently, from an ethical point of view, about a fetus when it's outside the womb rather than when it's inside the womb." Those are his quotes. Many children have been born severely premature and through the skills of good doctors and nurses they have developed and live normal lives today. Much time, energy and effort was spent exercising skills gained in medical school and in personal experience to save that little child's life. And yet, people will say it is all right to pull a fully formed child partially out of its mother's womb, suck its brains out and say that it was not a human because it was not fully born. That is an insult to the intelligence of any normal person.

From a social or societal perspective, forty-six million people have died since abortion was legalized. Thirty million of those would have been contributing members of society by now with their own children coming along. Analyze this: Think of the schools not built; think of the teachers not needed; think of the doctors and nurses and hospitals not needed. Think of the economic hit our country has taken because of abortion. Think also about one of the reasons Social Security is failing. Thirty million people would be contributing in some way to the social security fund, but they can't…they were aborted. Millions of them would be earning some of the highest wages of their lifetimes and helping to pay for the retirement of the older segment of society. I hate to bring it down to economics, but it helps paint the picture of the incumbent problems of abortion.

Another thing that is being affected is politics. The more liberal people wonder why the conservative base in America is growing stronger and stronger. I can tell you. The more liberal people tend to abort their children, their future voter base, while conservative people birth theirs and teach them that abortion is wrong and that we should always opt for life.

In fact, the normal human process is that a human will be produced after the fertilization of the egg unless unhindered nature intervenes. This is the way God designed us. It is not incumbent upon the Pro-Life position to prove anything because the normal process produces a life. It is incumbent upon the Pro-Choice movement to prove their statements concerning life and when it begins as well as its statements on when a person actually becomes a human worthy of protection. If they are unable to prove their position beyond doubt, then they must yield to the proof contained in the normal process of life which does not end in abortion but with a live birth.

I could go on, but I will not. Just let me say this: I am bound by the Word of God on this issue and all others. What it says and teaches, I must do. I am captive to the Word as Luther said. But I have observed this: *People will never be convinced by statistics or argument that abortion is wrong.* They will be convinced when it becomes a moral and spiritual issue with them and when they see that it is morally wrong. One thing that concerns me greatly is that the collective conscience of our nation does not seem to be bothered too much by the fact that over 46 million people have died since Roe v Wade, with the vast majority being for convenience.

Chapter 6

Let's Get Real

Two articles in the Thursday, September 1, 2005 edition of the *Augusta Chronicle* exhibit once more for us the startling power of the secular world view and how it has taken over the minds of the public. Where human beings and their origin are concerned, about 48 percent of the public thinks that Darwin was right and that the theory of evolution is the explanation for our existence. A few comments are in order.

First, consider the article entitled "Chimps' DNA is deciphered" with the subtitle of "discovery sheds light on humans." I quote the first and second paragraphs of this article from the Associated Press. "Scientists have deciphered the DNA of the chimpanzee, the closest living relative of humankind, and made comprehensive comparisons with the human genetic blueprint. It's a step toward finding a biological answer to a key question: What makes us human?" It continues, "There are no firm answers yet about how humans picked up key traits such as walking upright and developing complex language..."

The second article deals with the argument over creationism, evolution and intelligent design. Of course "intelligent design" is obviously a part of the idea that God created us and the entire world but scientists are seeking a way to express that all things were put together by a high form of intelligence without acknowledging God as the source of that intelligence. One scientist said: "We've got the catalog, now we just have to figure it out." Well… good luck!

The answers you are seeking will not be found in the comparison of the genetic codes of the chimpanzee and human beings. The first mistake the scientists are making is that DNA itself just happened. They actually believe that somehow all the combinations contained in the DNA came together to form a human being or any other creature or living thing. The odds against something like that happening are absolutely staggering. There is no human number which could be written which would adequately state such odds. And yet, scientists (who are supposed to be rational, educated people) accept these odds and assume that they have been overcome and have produced the genetic code.

The article on the genetic code further states that "humans and chimps have evolved separately since splitting from a common ancestor about 6 million years ago and their DNA remains highly similar…about 96 percent to almost 99 percent identical, depending on how the comparison is made." So, using the chimp DNA they say that they have uncovered several regions of human DNA that contain beneficial genetic changes which spread rapidly among humans within the past 250,000 years. One of those areas contains a gene called FOXP2 which involves acquiring speech. I have a question: Why is it that supposedly intelligent scientists would investigate the inferior to try to explain the superior? It seems to me that humans would have genetic information which explains our makeup that the chimp would not have. How can they assume certain things about humans by noticing what the chimp does not have? The process appears to be backward to me. Spiritually speaking, it is rather easy to discover what Satan is leading the secular mind to do. He is denigrating the superior and elevating the inferior. He never quits in his efforts against God. It all shows one the rationalizing power of Satan.

I wonder that if those odds concerning the chance of the DNA code just happening were translated into whether or not one of those scientists would be executed by a firing squad if they would still hold to them and use them as fact. It essentially costs them nothing to continue to feed this drivel to the public as scientific fact. They think nothing about asking us to believe that a bowl the size of the earth which contains only one black marble among quintillions of white marbles adequately explains the formation of our DNA. Someone blindfolded just happened to reach down into the center of that gigantic bowl and found the black marble on the first try. Now, come on...who is giving up their rational intelligence here?

Some scientists are beginning to understand how silly they sound when they try to convince the public of such things so they are now leaning toward "intelligent design" as their model. That is a step in the right direction but even then they don't want to give God the credit. They say that a "superior intelligence" is responsible but their secularism keeps them from crediting God. They are more prone to look to extraterrestrial intelligence as the source; you know, maybe someone from another planet or perhaps from another dimension. Yeah, sure, now that's completely believable. I can save these scientists all their trouble and at the same time save the taxpayers a lot of money by simply telling them what the answer is. Here's the answer to the whole question of how we became humans and how the chimpanzee became the chimpanzee. My answer also explains how the super-complex DNA code of all species is made up the way it is. Ready??? The Super Intelligence known as God made them that way. Now, isn't that simple? It is the only rational explanation but the secular world simply is not willing to accept that answer as the truth. They had rather bank on the one black marble among the quintillions of white marbles to explain it all. Again I say, I wonder if they would hold to those odds if their own lives were on the line. I don't think so.

The American public has been duped by these scientists to the point that 48 percent of them believe in the preposterous idea of evolution. Oh, yes, one other thing: It is scientifically impossible for life to spring from things which are not living. That is one of the laws of the universe. Nothing dead can produce life, but yet this is exactly what the evolutionist asks people to believe. Man has been struggling up the mountain of evolutionary thought and science for over one hundred years. One day he is going to reach the peak of that mountain and when the evolutionist reaches the summit he will find a prophet there waiting on him and that old prophet will be holding a Bible in his hand which says: "In the beginning God created the heaven and the earth."

Chapter 7

The Relevant Issue of Relevancy

There is a lot of discussion during these days about the issue of the relevancy of the Bible and subsequently of the church itself. It seems that most of this talk is coming from people who haven't been around long enough to have gained the insight needed to make some of their statements. The relevancy of the church is the "in" topic of today and we should be mature enough to realize that if the church goes where those who are espousing some of the things we must do to be relevant, then we will be far removed from what the Bible says about the nature of the church. Relevancy for the sake of relevancy is a black hole. It will suck the church down and thrust her into another "universe" of existence which will suit the world but will dilute the church to the point that she will be nothing but just another organization with good intentions.

When we speak of relevancy, we need to define exactly what we are talking about--*relevant as to what?* If the term means that the spiritual principles and doctrines of Scripture must be changed and shifted in order for them to be acceptable in society, then people need to realize something. The Bible is relevant to the solutions for our human condition only as long as it has not been changed to suit the ideas and desires of people who are looking for acceptance of the way they want to live. Scripture says that God's

Word is settled in heaven, (Ps. 119:89). It means that His Word is established and is a pillar in heaven. It can never change. If it could be changed, then God would cease to be God and that remains an impossibility. God only has to say something one time for it to be true forever. The unchanging God wrote the unchanging Word.

All human conditions are caused by basic spiritual problems. We have not invented anything new for which the Bible does not have an answer. But society is now calling for a Bible which will be relevant to the condition we now have in that it can be interpreted in such a fashion as to allow "wiggle room" for desired human activities. That is the erroneous application of relevancy. The bottom line is this: everything in our experience should be relevant to the Bible which in itself is the standard for human conduct and activities. We are not the standard by which the Bible is judged, but the Bible is the standard by which we are judged. Relevancy, where we and our desires are in view, should run in one direction from us to the Bible. If the Bible is going to be relevant to us, then of necessity it is we who must adjust because the Bible is constant and cannot change. If we ask the Bible to adjust or be relevant to society then we are placing a demand upon it that it cannot and will not meet. Jesus said; "These words are spirit and they are life"(John 6:63). They are applicable to all people of all times. They do not need to adjust for the times. They apply in any day and time.

The issue of relevancy and the church is a critical issue as well. We must not compromise holiness to be relevant to this world, and we are skirting dangerously close to that in today's church. For us to be able to read the Bible and get our instructions upon which we are built, it had to be set in a historical context. But, that does not mean that the spiritual principles and truths of God's working with us and in us is locked into a particular historical time line and perspective. The application of the Bible's truths is for anyone at any time in the history of the world because "these words are spirit and they are life." That is why the Bible is always relevant. And that is why the church must be careful of the things it does in order to call itself relevant. Being relevant is not a problem with those who adhere to biblical doctrines and the proper focus for the church. Those who want to take the church into strange waters find they have to adopt a secular meaning for relevancy to convince people that they are legitimate. Remember, if by relevant we are saying that the church must change itself in order to attract society, then we are living in a danger zone. We must remember that the church, which is the Body of Christ, *is relevant* to the human condition of lostness and, after one is saved, to holiness.

The real problem is that people in today's world expect that the church should be all things to all people. It should be meeting every need of mankind, and if it doesn't then it is no longer relevant. I would point out that the church was never meant to meet all the needs of humankind. I restate it this way: "if, by relevant, we mean that the Bible is sufficient for our needs and stands as the answer for us in all days and in all times, then we are correct. But, if by relevant, we mean that the Bible and the church must change in order to satisfy our viewpoints and desires in order to be effective then we are wrong. We do wrong when we assume or expect the church to submit itself to the demands of society in order to have value.

The church is relevant to this society and time in that its unchanging message can be applied in any day and time. It is always relevant to any society in that respect. But, if we expect that relevancy means to be like the society in order to be accepted and valued then we are holding an unacceptable position. It would do us well to remember that the church is the Body of Christ. It is governed by certain spiritual principles which cannot change. If we want the Body of Christ to adjust itself in order for us to feel good about what we do in our society and personal lives, then we are setting ourselves up as the authority and expecting the Body of Christ to be pleased with that. We are the ones who must do the adjusting, not the Scripture and not the church either (as long as the church is being obedient to the Scripture itself). Today, we are seeing that a church is judged to be successful or not by the way it adjusts itself to get the most people to attend. The more it modifies itself to make the world feel comfortable, then the "better" it is. But, the more it holds to the old truths and remains separate from the world, the more irrelevant it is deemed to be.

This writer is amused at those who are supposedly setting the trend with the contemporary movement. This movement is built upon the premise that the church is relevant only so long as it changes to satisfy the demands of what society says is worship. These leaders, while touting their innovations and originality, all look and act basically the same. They do the same things. They wear the same wardrobe configurations. They fix their hair the same way. They remind me of the hippies of the sixties who wanted to be different from society but all wound up looking the same. They adopt the same basic approach to change a church from what it was to their particular style by adopting a "model" that is supposed to automatically produce "success."

And, it might be noted that many Southern Baptist churches have been split with devastating results over this issue. All of this is being done so the church can be relevant, hip, innovative and "with it." Many churches have been disrupted, divided and sometimes virtually destroyed because someone, usually a new incoming preacher, has basically forced what he considers to be a new and relevant model upon them. This writer has kept a list of such situations and is familiar with at least fifteen churches so affected. The list is still growing as news of other disruptions make their way to me. This brings us to the question: Is the church the Body of Christ which should be what He wants it to be or is it an organization to be "designed" in such a way as to be acceptable and "relevant" to the secular society?

I would like to remind the readers that the Body of Christ is constant in its focus and purpose, and we should be very careful about what we decide it should be doing in order for the world to be attracted to it. Just remember this: A crowd is not necessarily a church. There is a vast difference between the two, and we might note that it was a crowd that followed Jesus into Jerusalem singing

His praises and then called for His crucifixion only a short time later. Crowds are not loyal. They are content only so long as they are happy.

I will not belabor the "contemporary" issue any longer. Suffice it to say, that it does relate to the relevancy issue to a great degree. I am aware that some will agree with this commentary, and some will not like it at all. Most who will disagree probably will be younger men who do not yet have the maturity or experience to understand the full ramifications of what I have been stating. As time goes by, they will understand it better. In the meantime they need to give me the same right to disagree with them in their approaches that they assume by labeling those who do not follow their model as out of touch and irrelevant. Time will tell who is right and, as for me, I plan to let the Lord build His church as I remain faithful to the biblical principles it is built upon - namely preaching the gospel, edifying the saints and ministering to those in need.

Chapter 8

The Integrity of Christianity

When God made man, He placed within him the desire to worship, with the plan being that man would worship God Himself. This basic principle which was placed in man has been corrupted like everything else that the human race has ever touched. The fact that man desires to worship *something* has been corrupted to the point that he will worship *anything*, and this is not what God had in mind. The presence of the myriad of cults proves that anything will do for worship as far as humans are concerned. But, the principle has not changed where God is concerned. He still will not be pleased unless we are worshipping Him properly, and herein lays a grave danger to Christianity in today's world.

We all know that there are a number of denominations that have varying degrees of differences in the way we view things. The fact that differences exist expresses the many and varied ways in which humans think about things. But, the primary fact we must remember is that we can allow others to disagree with us on issues as long as those issues are peripheral and not those which are dealing with salvation itself. When a denomination or group holds to issues which do dishonor to the work of Jesus Christ on the Cross of Calvary or when their views completely disavow something which is critical to salvation, then their hand should be

45

called on the issue, and they should be held responsible. Now, this writer knows what the field of play is like. No one dares to question others because if they do, they might be considered divisive and hateful. I think that we have come so far into heresy and bad practices that the time has come for people to be held accountable for what they do and say which promote confusion and misunderstanding about Christianity.

If I were a lost person reflecting on the possibility of becoming a Christian, and if I were to base my decision on what I see on television today on some "Christian" programs, I would conclude that I would not want to be a Christian. Even lost people have the ability to discern when something is not right. They can easily spot a con man, and they don't want to have anything to do with them. Sadly, too many people who are standing before a crowd of people proclaiming a message are leading those people astray by bad doctrine and bad practices. Christianity is being erroneously defined in the minds of a gullible and spiritually blind public in a way which is poles apart from what the Bible says is the true nature of our most holy faith. The Apostle Paul would not recognize what is going on since there is no biblical precedent for some of the beliefs and for most of the things that these people are doing.

Of course, if any of them read this commentary, they will declare that the writer is "'mean spirited" and divisive. I really don't care what they say because the time has come when people like myself and others must stand up and demand that the practices of people selling themselves as Christian ministers must be cleaned up or they should expect to be revealed for what they are: religious con men who are leading people down the primrose path of error and confusion. The primary goal of these "preachers" is the very thing which drives just about everything that happens in the world today: $$$$. I would never take such an approach to a person or denomination that differs with me on baptism, for example, as long as that baptism was not looked upon as a work of salvation itself. I would never formulate an argument against a denomination that has a different view of church government than we Baptists do although I would disagree with them.

But the level of practice I am discussing in this commentary is far beyond those things. What is happening today is heresy. It is demeaning to biblical Christianity, and it is leading millions of people to expect the wrong things from a saving relationship with Christ. He did not come so that we would never be physically ill as a human. He did not come so that we could be assured of financial prosperity. He did not come so that we could display so called activities of the Spirit which stand totally against Scripture. These people have even developed a new vocabulary concerning faith and practice that is never mentioned in the biblical record and is never alluded to by any biblical author. The idea of "sowing a seed" has been taken and extrapolated into something that is absolutely ridiculous. It works for them as evidenced by the fact that they all use the ploy. "Send in your seed offering today, and God will reward you in multiples." "Sow a fifty dollar per month seed so that God can bring you your harvest." It seems to me that all those people who are sowing all those seeds need to take a good look at the fact that the only ones riding in Mercedes automobiles and building multimillion dollar "parsonages" are the "preachers" themselves. All the others keep coming to the arena and "hoping" for their miracle, or else they are there to watch a professional "performer" manipulate an audience. They have been duped into believing that anything they cannot understand is proof of the presence of the Holy Spirit. Nothing could be further from the truth.

When I watch certain faith healers, I am embarrassed for the true Christians in the land. I am embarrassed that their faith is being so portrayed before the world. Sincere Christians have spent their lives on the mission field in dangerous situations, and it has not been for the "brand" of Christianity espoused by the likes of some of the prosperity preachers. The on-stage antics are demeaning to biblical Christianity, and responsible people in places of influence should start making them answer for their actions. When sincere people go witness to the lost, they often have to overcome the image of Christianity which the person has absorbed because of T.V. hucksters. No biblical precedent for "blowing" on people, causing them to fall out exists. Similarly, no biblical precedent can be found for waving one's arm toward a group of people making them all fall back. Nor is there biblical evidence to warrant touching a person on the forehead and causing him or her to swoon. All of this, of course, is attributed to "the presence of the Holy Spirit". God's Spirit is not the author of confusion. Nevertheless, what is done in the meetings of many of these so-called "faith and prosperity" preachers brings nothing but confusion to the minds of thinking people.

Watching Christian television becomes dreary and depressing. One will not have to wait very long until confronted with exactly what I am speaking about. The prosperity preachers are very successful in their gathering of other's "seeds" as evidenced by the fact that they can afford to dominate the very expensive television time so completely. As stated earlier, a casual perusal of the television fare and of printed materials by some of these people will reveal exactly what I am addressing in this commentary.

And, is there some spiritual "law" which is affecting so many of those on "Christian" television and which is keeping them from looking and acting like normal, godly, decent people? The "performance" aspect of the whole thing has led many preachers, and singers to adopt the wildest "look" in the world. The men look like clowns or shady used car dealers, and the women would pass for a prostitute in almost any setting. I know that I am saying things which many people think and speak of privately, but we must begin to deal with all of this or else resign ourselves to the fact that our faith, Christianity, is being redefined in the minds of people such that they are adopting something which is totally alien to biblical Christianity or else they are turning away from our faith altogether.

Christianity's focus on grace and kindness has opened the door for people to practice just about anything in its name and not be called into question. Remember this: *Grace does not mean weakness and neither does it mean acquiescence to that which is wrong.* Jesus stood up to those who were teaching the wrong things. He did not assume the position that most people have in this modern day and let heresy continue unabated in order to be "kind." I think He would have us stand up and demand that the faith He died to establish must be protected. As I said earlier, I can hear it now, "God will judge anyone who speaks out against this ministry." I don't think so. I think He has been waiting for someone and hopefully more, to speak out and stop some of the ridiculous activity which has been taking place in the name of Jesus. We have come so far into this situation until we will have to go further than we would like to go in order to bring things back to normal. The integrity of Christianity is at stake, and responsible people and groups must stand up and be counted on the issue of purity. We owe that, and much more, to Jesus.

Chapter 9

The Declension of the
United States of America

In Webster's Dictionary, the word "declension" is as follows: "A falling off towards a worse state; a downward tendency; deterioration; decay." It perfectly describes what is happening to the United States right before our eyes. We are literally watching a society decline into the abyss of immorality at a more rapid rate than one could have imagined only a few years ago. In fact, it is happening so fast that it leaves one's head spinning as we strive to find where the moral fulcrum is located on any given day.

When one reads some of the history of the Roman Empire they can get somewhat of a glimpse as to where we are headed as a nation. The Roman Empire fell as a direct result of immorality among its citizenry. This immoral frame of mind polluted every aspect of their society which was the most powerful empire in the world at that time. It polluted the home and caused the destruction of the Roman family. Immorality polluted their government and caused it to lose its focus and effectiveness. It polluted the men in their military and caused it to become ineffective and less powerful than before. It weakened their resolve to be the nation and people they had been before. The Roman army is infamous for its cruelty and that was a direct result of the devaluing of human life. Chaos reigned in the Roman social order from the Emperor to the common people. Yes, immorality caused the decay of that great society. Even at that, we learn from history that it took a long period of time for the Roman Empire to actually fall to such levels that it ceased to be an empire. It did not happen quickly in the span of only a few years or decades. But, they are gone, and the American people need to examine exactly what happened to them, and then they need to recognize the parallels that are present in our country.

The great Grecian Empire is another case in point. It was totally democratic with the people having absolute control over the direction of the country. They were totally free, and when a people are totally free they will descend into anarchy and rebellion. If man does not have some constraints upon himself, he will finally destroy himself and the society of which he is a part. The Greek Empire produced some of the greatest minds that have ever existed on planet earth. These people produced some of the most wonderful literature and philosophy that has ever emerged. Societies have always reflected on the teachings of Plato and the writings of Homer as well as others. It was a brilliant society, but it too was corrupted from within. The same immorality which destroyed the Romans also destroyed the Greeks. Today, they are a nation with no empire and very little influence in the world. I'm sure they thought that a general declension of their nation would never happen to them, but it did. Anytime a person, a people or a nation slides down the slippery slope into immorality, it dooms them to destruction. The British Empire is a more modern example of how a once powerful nation can so radically decline because of immorality within. The roadways of history are strewn with the debris of many nations which have ceased to exist as powerful entities simply because of the inward decay of immorality. No nation of history was any worse at the point of immorality than is the United States. What makes this country think that they face any different future than others who have traveled our present path? We should be taking good lessons from history and correcting some of the deadly influences which destroyed others. But, it seems that such a course will not be taken. It seems that, with our eyes wide open, America is on a death march into declension which will ultimately mask us little more than a footnote in history books as some other nations are.

Immorality in every form has become the entertainment and desire of so many of the people of the United States. Things are happening now that one would never have dreamed of only five years ago. I want to mention just a few things.

1. The redefining of marriage is a serious threat to our society. It strikes at the family which is the ordered heart of any society. Who would have thought even one year ago that such an abomination would happen in our country as to declare that two people of the same sex could "marry" each other? That was something that one would never have dreamed would happen. And, such things are happening so rapidly that it is stunning the nation. Did you ever think you would see the day when homosexuals would proudly proclaim their immoral lifestyle before the nation the way they do today? Did you ever think that it would be our courts which are filled with activist judges which are actually winning the battle for the gay agenda? The ramifications of the decision by the Supreme Court of Massachusetts are astounding when one thinks about it.

With the ACLU threatening people and activist judges providing the proper impetus, just where will this all stop? It is frightening to think about. I think that when something of such importance is considered and when something of such far-reaching implications for a society is dealt with, the people themselves should make the decision and not just a few people on a court who seemingly have lost all common sense. But, those pushing the homosexual agenda have been smart enough to know that they would fail if it was left up to the people so their strategy has been to change the venue of decision making from the public to the courts. So, then, just a few people who sit on our courts are moving this immoral agenda forward to the consternation of the people who really should be the ones to make the decision on the issue. Polls show that even in

Massachusetts, the vast majority of the people do not want same sex marriages. These people, with the help of radical liberal lawyers and judges will not stop at Massachusetts. They will come to Georgia and every other state in an effort to see just how far they can go with the normalization of same sex marriages and their homosexual agenda. Only God knows what the final chapter will read like.

2. The emergence of the Judiciary as a legislative body. The United States is in danger of being radically transformed through the use of the judicial system as a method of re-interpreting the laws to make them fit the agenda and mindset of the judges. The original intent of the judiciary and the judges which occupy their office was to make sure that the laws involved in a particular case were followed correctly. They were to be the ones who made sure that the law was equally applied. About sixty years ago the scene changed in that the judges began to see their task as something quite different. Slowly but surely they began to interpret the law the way they saw it as it applied to a particular situation. In other words, the application of the law began to "float" according to the different particulars of a case. Once this was accepted and written into an "opinion", it then set a precedent for the next case to which the opinion could be applied. Over a period of time, the original law which was supposed to be judiciously applied by the judges became something which hardly resembled the law in its original intent.

This is what is happening to the constitution. It has now been described as a "living document" which can be "re-adjusted" in its application in order to meet almost any criteria. This allows for activists and judges who are sympathetic to their causes to formulate an application of a law or constitutional statement which totally misses the point and which is a misuse of the original intent of the constitutional authors. If the people of the United States do not stand up and demand that this sort of thing stop, then they are at the mercy of a handful of people who can actually re-write law to fit their own agenda or understanding of it instead of judiciously applying it. The liberal agendas which are so aggressive these days would not have a chance without the judges. A small group of people are negating the work of congress in many ways and they are telling the whole of society what their mores should be like. This is not right and must stop. Originally the different branches of the government were designed to check and balance each other to keep one from becoming too powerful. The Executive branch had veto power but a veto could also be overridden by the Legislative branch. Those two still balance each other. The Legislative branch has a power it is not exercising, and therefore the Judiciary is running wild unchecked. The Legislative branch can, if it would, instruct the Judiciary that they cannot rule concerning certain things. This is supposed to balance the power of the Judiciary but it is not being employed. I think the American people should demand that the Legislative branch exercise this right given to them in our constitution. Without this balance, the Judiciary will continue to warp the law to fit their liking. It will also re-shape the moral code of the United States into something which is a total abomination.

3. The media has become a six-hundred pound immoral gorilla which is bound, bent and determined to foist all the immorality on the general public they can. Actually, they are insulting the intelligence of the American public by assuming that they will only watch or purchase those things which are immoral in some way. I am referring not only to Hollywood, but to the giant television media as well which is piping the grossest forms of immorality right into our living rooms. Recent huge successes of Christian films should show these people that the public wants something different. Good secular family films have also enjoyed wonderful box office receipts. But the media giants seem blind to this fact. They continually offer only those things that reflect their own perverted lifestyles. Seemingly, they do not have a good moral frame of reference with which to create anything. In the past thirty years or so things, they have degenerated at an alarming rate. Things are shown on television now that one would never have imagined in prior years. The minds and hearts of a couple of generations have been poisoned by what they have seen and heard. The time is quickly approaching when Christian people and moral people of other faiths will have to turn off their television sets in order to maintain their own conscience in a proper manner.

The national news media is going to have to bear the burden of much of the declension of America. They are like a bunch of mangy vultures sitting on an old dead tree just waiting to find something that stinks enough for them so that they can swoop down and gorge themselves. I have lost all respect for the national news media. Their behavior in the last two to three years is despicable. The American public has been force fed a twenty-four-hour-a-day diet of news which is slanted toward a liberal interpretation of events. It shows the same things over and over with the result that people are indoctrinated in the direction the political agenda of the particular media is slanted. Their coverage of political things in particular betrays their liberal viewpoint. And, if an event does not suit their need, they simply ignore it or pay only as much attention to it as they can get by with.

Also, too much is told. There must be some things which are not for public consumption such as military secrets. Our news media sits in their studios and enables our enemies to know exactly what we are doing and what their own aggression has done to us. If they see that something has worked, they will simply do it again. It is absolutely foolish for the media to divulge as much information as they do. Of course they are after one thing: advertising dollars and ratings. All else to them is not much of a consideration. In my humble opinion, the media of today are at the very core of a lot of our societal ills. It has, however, been encouraging to see the FCC begin to reign the mass media in on some counts. Notice though, that the media is screaming to high heaven that their "right" to say things and do certain things is being infringed upon. Our society is crumbling morally and the mass media is contributing highly to that crumble while laughing all the way to the bank. Some moral sanity must be restored.

4. The church in America is in a mess generally. The denominations showing growth are those which adhere to the Bible and teach their people those principles found therein. The real problem is that too many preachers and church leaders are too politically correct to deal with the truth. They are afraid they will offend someone and it seems that the worse thing one can do to another in today's PC world is to offend them or tell them they are wrong in some way. So, where moral issues become political ones, those preachers abdicate their position and modify their message in order for it to fit the will and desires of a PC world. I believe that one of the major reasons our nation is in a moral abyss is because the preachers of righteousness have ceased to do just that, and they have altered their message to be palatable to a world which hates God and His Authority: The Bible.

Passages which make a definite statement on issues such as homosexuality are reinterpreted to fit the agenda of the homosexuals. Anyone who says they are called of God and who will not stand for the Word of God and the moral positions prescribed in it is not worth the salt in their blood and should be honest enough to step out of the pulpit and go get himself an honest job. The Episcopal Church as well as the Methodist and Presbyterian Church in the USA, joined by the United Churches of Christ and others can't even find due north on the moral compass enough to know where they should stand on homosexuality. If I were a member of any of those denominations, I would repent, beg God for forgiveness and join another denomination which honors Him. These churches are fast becoming some of that immoral refuse left alongside the road of history. God will not honor them as they do not honor Him, and He will see to it that they cease to be at some point in time. Millions of good people are being led astray by these who are nothing more than the biblical "blind leading the blind." God will exact His judgment upon these people in due time. What America needs is for God's men to stand boldly and proclaim His truths while relying on Him for protection. We must have a rebirth of biblical preaching if we are to return to a solid foundation morally and spiritually. What we really need is another Great Awakening and a national revival. Pray that God will send us one.

This writer has only pointed to a few of the most vital areas in The Declension of the United States. There are many areas which are rapidly declining such as the value of life and the emergence of pornography as a form of entertainment. We are becoming more like Europe every day. The rest of the world looks at the U.S. and scoffs at our puritanical viewpoints. I think that speaks volumes about how far they have fallen if they thing we are puritanical. The declension of the United States is thoroughly under way and it is not akin to a freight train which is out of control and headed for a disastrous wreck. God help us to turn to Him before it is too late.

Chapter 10

Needed: Defenders of Morality

Recently the Supreme Court of the United States rendered another one of those rulings which defy logic and morality. They ruled that a law which outlawed virtual pornography was unconstitutional and therefore it should be overturned thus allowing the pornographers to create virtual pornography which depicts children in pornographic ways. They are more concerned about the rights of the pornographer than they are about standing in the gap and becoming protectors of a decent, moral society. I think that every citizen has more of a right to expect that their environment will be protected than the immoral purveyors of pornographic films have to do their wicked business. The Supreme Court got the issues confused and missed a golden opportunity to use their position to protect the environment of the good moral citizens of America. Their opinion now, in effect becomes law and their opinion let the wrong group of people win. Question: Do the good, moral, Godly people of society have a right to expect our courts and judges to protect and preserve our environment or, instead, should they simply accept the fact that the court allowed the base and immoral to flourish?

We have become so "rights" oriented in this society until we are about to destroy ourselves. With every right comes a corresponding responsibility and when people want rights without responsibilities as the pornographers do, the good citizenry should expect that our leaders would step up and defend what is good and not what is immoral. They should help create a society which blesses its citizens rather than curses them. Shall they be the protector and defender of a decent and moral society as we should expect of them, or are they going to get so sidetracked by the "rights" issue as to allow the immoral to destroy us? So the Supreme Court got the issues confused. They have myopia when it comes to rulings which involve rights. The immoral and criminal elements of society rejoiced at the day when the venue concerning their desired activities shifted to the "rights" arena and away from the morality arena. If they could get their cause to be interpreted as a "right" then they would have even the courts on their side and this is exactly what has happened. It may be a "right" granted by the court to create virtual pornography, but it is not a right to degenerate society and this is where the court went wrong in their "opinion" forming process.

But, the average citizen has given up this ground. They have bought into the "rights" issue and when those "rights" are appealed to then the good citizen simply throws up his hands and gives up the formation of his society to the interpretation of the court. Yes, the immoral and criminal elements loved it when the scene changed and their activities could then be considered a "right". They knew they didn't have to fight the fight; the courts would do it for them, and they do. All they have to do is get their issue to court in some sort of appeal and then the judges write law from the bench and become social engineers instead of judges.

The ruling on virtual pornography which was handed down by the Supreme Court must make every thinking citizen feel that the collective intelligence of the Supreme Court is hovering somewhere around what, on a thermometer, is absolute O. And, since they are issuing "opinions", is there some rule somewhere which banishes moral considerations from the agenda? Are those championing a moral society and the stability it brings supposed to sit quietly and silently in the corner since someone has appealed to the "rights" issue on something such as virtual pornography?

I am concerned that anyone who has thought these things through would say that virtual pornography is victimless porn. There is no such thing as an immoral act or a criminal act being victimless. Someone pays the price for that kind of behavior. That is simply God's moral law for the universe. So, as some would suggest, is it different when virtual people or children are watched performing pornographic acts? It is hard to tell the virtual people from real ones or else the pornographers would not be interested in it. Those making such videos or movies are morally bankrupt and those using them are just as morally degenerate. Would a person watch such virtual pornography unless it gratified the same basic passions which real people would gratify? I think not. So this victimless porn or victimless crime reasoning is flawed to the core.

The parameters for the social and moral life of the United States is now being rewritten by liberal judges and we, the citizenry, have been conditioned to accept their rulings as the last word. There must come a time when we would stand up and fight for a moral society. We simply must not "roll over and play dead". Do we really have to accept the ruling that virtual child pornography is "artistic expression"? I think it is an insult to the intelligence of our people to think we would accept this. Anyone with a modicum of intelligence knows when something is art and when it has crossed the line.

In addition, child pornography is illegal and the purveyors of this filth think they have now found a way around the law by using virtual children and adults in their films. And, the court aids and abets the degeneration of society by issuing a ruling so centered on "rights" that the protection of society is forgotten. If the court is going to say that, in their opinion, a person has the right to push his immorality on society, then the court should be responsible for setting some boundaries and responsibilities on those "rights". I think it would be good for upright, moral citizens everywhere to write their representatives in Washington and urge them to write a law so tight that the pornographers would never be able to find a loophole.

It must be remembered that simply because something has been declared legal by the Supreme Court does not mean it is moral. Abortion is legal, but it is not moral. Gambling is legal, but not moral. Being a drunkard is legal, but not moral. And, virtual child pornography may be legal according to this Supreme Court ruling but it is not moral. There is one thing the Supreme Court should bear in mind: They might hold court on earth, but they do not hold session in heaven. They might create the environment in which the immoral pornographer can flourish, but they have not changed the fact that it is wrong is the eyes of Him who watches all of our actions.

Chapter 11

A Major Deterrent to Revival

There has been much discussion lately about the fact that revival is desperately needed in our churches and in our land at large. Many have been lamenting the fact that the revivals of yesteryear which had such an effect on our society at large are not occurring today. "If we could only have another Great Awakening, a general national revival, we would be all right as a country" is what we hear people saying. There is a growing awareness of the fact that nothing short of a true national revival will rescue our nation. America has fallen so low spiritually and morally that we cannot rescue ourselves. Our politicians don't know what to do with the mess we have created. So, more and more, people are acknowledging that a national, God-sent revival is necessary to preserve the land and rebuild the moral and spiritual strength of America.

May I suggest what I believe to be one of the major deterrents to a revival occurring in America in this day and time? *Revival is being deterred in America today because of our multicultural makeup which has become the politically correct model for us to follow.* Let me be quick to point out the obvious: America has always welcomed people from all cultures to come to these shores and enjoy the freedom we possess and prosperity we possess. During the late 1800's and the early 1900's Ellis Island welcomed millions into this country, and we found strength in those people. They came here to work and make a new life for themselves, and most of them succeeded in that venture. But, those people came here to be Americans. They, by and large, adopted the frame of mind about being American which bonded them to all others. They joined the family and were welcomed. For them to come here and maintain their own nationality and foreign way of life was not something that the mass of these people saw themselves doing. They were becoming American. They were not coming to these shores in order to have a free place to bring their own society in among us and never change anything about their lives. The Chinese as well as the Germans, Italians and Jews all had "pockets" where their former culture was predominant but they saw themselves as operating within the scope of American life.

In today's *politically correct environment* (PC) we have something quite different. Ethnic groups feel that they can move into America and maintain their culture. They see America as just another geographical place where their culture exists. There is little thought of changing and adopting American ways of life. Their customs are never changed at all. Their dress is unaffected even though it separates them from the society at large. Their language remains the same with no desire to make English their primary language. So, what we have is a multicultural society which is quickly losing its primary identity because our leaders are not setting a standard as to what is expected from those who come here. Multiculturalism will destroy a country because, after so long a time, the country no longer knows exactly who it is.

We should demand that those who come to America learn the English language. One symptom of our danger is easily observed in that we change the roadway signs to reflect both the Hispanic and English instructions. This is America, and I think they should be printed in English. When a person calls most companies today they will be instructed to press a certain digit on the phone if they want to hear the instructions in English. That is backward. If a person wanted to hear instructions in Spanish, they should be the ones to press a certain digit. The first instructions given over the phone is in Spanish and then the English speaking person is told to stay on the line if they want English. Something is wrong here. It mirrors what we are doing in America. We are accommodating multiculturalism. We simply are too sensitive and feelings oriented to tell a person that they are different from the society at large and that they need to adjust. We don't want to commit the greatest crime of today which is hurting someone's feelings.

The same is true of religion. The people who come to America should understand that we are a Christian nation. We were founded upon Christianity and the Judeo-Christian principles found in the Bible. All a person has to do is to go read our founding documents and read the statements of many of our founding fathers. There is no one who is intellectually honest who could come to any other conclusion. Yet other religions are invited to come here and worship with freedom. We welcome them and give them the American right to freedom of religion. But Christianity is being crowded out by the other world religions. We can't function as we always have in the past because of the PC idea that if even one person is offended by something we do, we must cease to do it. If I travel into a Muslim country and attend a meeting, I would expect that a Muslim prayer would be offered. I would not be offended by that since I should expect that that would be the case. But in America, which was founded as a Christian nation, we are no longer free to pray openly in any venue because we have adopted the PC model of multiculturalism, and we might hurt someone else's feelings in some way if we pray in the name of Jesus. They came to America. They should expect that it would be so.

Now, let's get to the revival question. In the past, when a revival came in America or in an area, it was a Christian revival since the preponderance of people was Christian. So, since most of society identified itself as Christian, everyone came closer to responding to the effects of the revival, and therefore a Christian revival occurred. But today, if we have a Christian revival, much of society will be unmoved. Because of our multiculturalism, which in large part expresses itself in the religious realm, large segments of society will remain unaffected or uncaring about the revival. If the Christians were revived, that is only a portion of the societal makeup. Much of the nation would be unmoved. They are maintaining their own religions with Christianity being classed as no more than one among many. It is no longer viewed as the predominant religion of America and has been relegated to another status. If the Christians in the 1700's and 1800's as well as the first half of the 1900's had a revival, then the whole nation was affected. But today much of the nation would hardly pay us any attention. We have failed to hold Christianity up as the religion upon which the founding documents of this nation were grounded.

So, revival such as has been seen in the past probably won't happen again apart from a mighty act of God. We should pray that God would supernaturally intervene and bring a national revival to our midst. That is the only thing which is going to save this great country. The pagan religions living among us know nothing about revival but Christians do, and we should pray and pray that God would bless us with a heaven sent national revival.

Chapter 12

Confronting a Decadent Culture

For two hundred years, America has been recognized as the moral and spiritual leader of the world. Even today, with all of its wickedness and imperfections, our great country is still considered to be the moral bellwether of the world. It hardly seems possible, but the people of other countries all over the world actually look up to us for moral leadership. I think that this says something very disturbing about the moral and spiritual condition of the world at large because we know that our moral quality is declining rapidly. In fact, we have fallen to new lows in our personal morality. If left to itself a society will degenerate very rapidly into a people mired in the filthiest moral quagmire. Things are happening today which were unheard of or not thought of until the recent past.

Our founding fathers would be astounded if they knew how people have used their founding documents to pervert the morality and spirituality of the American public. Our U.S. Constitution is now being interpreted by a society dominated by secular humanists and liberals. One may wonder why some of the constitutional rulings which have been handed down over the past few years sound so weird and convoluted. I think the answer is an easy one. A document written by God-fearing Christian and deist writers is being twisted out of shape and form in an effort to make it apply to the demands of a liberal, secular society dominated by people who care very little about spiritual matters.

The First Amendment has been abused by these same people to the point that they claim that it makes room for pornography and sacrilegious expression. Indecency is now supposed to fall under the First Amendment and anyone with a sound mind knows that it should not be so. Christianity is a favorite target for abuse, and when it occurs it is supposed to be acceptable under some twisted interpretation of the First Amendment. John Quincy Adams said: "We have no government armed in power capable of contending with human passions unbridled by morality and religion. Our constitution was made *only* for a moral and religious people. It is *wholly inadequate* for the government of any other" (emphasis mine). And, that is the very reason the constitutional rulings are sounding so absurd today. They are trying to reinterpret a document made for a godly people and make it apply to liberal, secular, godless situations.

Thomas Jefferson made this statement: "No nation has yet existed or been governed without religion, nor can be. The Christian religion is the best religion that has been given to man and as Chief Magistrate of this nation I am bound to give it the sanction of my example." I only wish we had leaders who felt that way today. Our former President, Bill Clinton, made this comment while speaking to a meeting of homosexual activists. He said, "We are redefining in practical terms the immutable ideals that have guided us from the beginning." It is clear that he wants to remake society into something the founding fathers did not foresee. Incidentally, if the ideals are immutable then they are *unchangeable*. Somehow I think the former President of the United States ought to know that.

The church must stand against the spirit of its age if we are to be a moral and spiritual lighthouse at all. Ships crash upon the rocks when the light in the lighthouse goes out. I'm concerned that instead of challenging the spirit of our age, the church is absorbing that spirit, and as she does, the light in the lighthouse grows dimmer and dimmer. The only entity which has a true message of hope is the church. Trillions have been spent pursuing the promises and hopes of the government and politicians, but society is in an ever-worsening condition. Where moral and spiritual guidance is lacking or watered down with secularism, the lowest common denominator of human conduct will prevail. Each generation can only teach its children the level of moral conduct it has experienced itself. But, it is easy for each generation to slip just a little more into the moral abyss. So, therefore, the continual trend of society is downward.

Somehow this must be confronted and reversed, and the church is the only institution which has the moral power to do so. We must meet the challenge. We have no option but to continue to try to survive in an ever-decaying environment. And while I know what Scripture says about how man is going to get worse and worse until the end comes, I do not think we can sit on our laurels, enjoy our spiritual security and watch the world go by. That is not why God has kept us here. There are those to be saved, and each one who is saved will have a different morality and spirituality with which to impact this society in a godly way. Our primary task is the redemption of the lost, but once that has happened then obedience is the issue. God is still on the throne of the universe, and we are still His church. We must remain faithful to the task set before us because, I believe, that we are the last bastion of morality and godliness. If we fail there is absolutely no hope for this nation. So, the church must stand up and confront a decadent culture. She is the only one empowered with the message which will succeed and the only one empowered with the Holy Spirit of God who has equipped her for the task.

Chapter 13

A Solid Constant

The world in which we live today is fraught with all kinds of problems our fathers and grandfathers never dreamed of. Every direction in which we turn seems to hold new and threatening surprises for people in these days. The economy is a source of a great deal of anxiety for many people with the stock market bouncing around the way it does, and the general direction of the bounce has been downward. Many people who had quite a nest egg are finding that their finances are squeezed tighter than ever. Others who have investments and who have been depending on them for retirement are now having to work jobs until things, hopefully, rebound somewhat. These are stressful times where the economy is concerned.

Now, we find that our safety in our own country is not as secure as it once was. Since September 11, 2001 things have changed drastically. The news media is constantly talking about the threat against our country and Americans abroad. We have given so much to the world, and yet we are the most hated by many countries. The threat from Islamic militants is a real one not only here but in other countries as well. Every day we are bombarded with news about probable strikes and attacks. We are told to be careful and to have contingency plans in case certain things happen. The stress builds in the lives of people and it is affecting the way we think and act within our own country.

In addition to the things already mentioned, it seems that our own society is coming apart at the seams. We are now coping with a generation raised on heavy metal music, rebellion and drugs. Illicit sex is sold to the public on television and on the movie screen, and we wonder why our young people think things which were formally unspeakable are now things which they should not be denied. The general moral climate of America is at a new low, and it seems to be heading even lower as the base instincts of a degenerate society are being fed even more of the poison which has already caused a titanic shift in who we are and how we conduct ourselves.

But there is one thing which does not change. There is one constant in society to which our people can go for peace and assurance. *The church, which is the spiritual body of Christ, is a spiritual organism which has the answers for the problems in society.* It is ultimately the place to which most people finally turn for guidance and comfort. Even people who have never given God a turn in life want to go to the church for comfort when death comes. They want a man of God to say a few words of comfort. They ultimately want to think that the message of salvation proclaimed by the church applies to them and their loved ones. The church is the only institution on the earth with the proper answers for life. No other institution or organization deals with eternal life. No one else has the message the church possesses. Wall Street deals with money. The American Bar Association deals with the law. The courts deal with dispensing justice. Medical institutions deal with keeping people healthy. But *no one else but the Church deals with the eternal life factor, the most important factor of all.* When frustration and anxiety come and when the pressure and stresses of life come to bear, no one can offer the comfort, peace, solitude, assurance and love that the Church has to offer. A sinful world will look everywhere for the answers to life except the place God has designed to help them. People will trust a little pill in a bottle to calm their lives more than they will trust Jesus who can completely straighten them out and bring true peace.

Just remember. When life's burdens and frustrations come to bear on you, there is a place that cares. The people who make up the church are the ones a person can depend on for help. The Lord of the Church is the one they can look to for salvation and true peace. Commit your life to Jesus Christ, God's answer to our human condition. Hold the church high. Lift her up. Invest your life in the spiritual body of Christ, the church, and you will find that there is peace in the midst of this storm we call the human experience.

Chapter 14

The Holiness of Worship

There has never been a day in which the church needed to take a stand and challenge society more than it does today. The people of the world will not respect the Christian faith unless they see those of us who claim to be Christians setting a standard which challenges them. If we conduct ourselves like the world does, then why would the world listen to anything we have to say on spiritual issues? What is needed in today's world is a church standing for what is right, not necessarily for what is popular or politically correct.

What we are finding today is that, in order to attract the people to a church and in order to have large numbers, churches are lowering the bar to such a low standard that the people of the world can step over it without ever feeling challenged or confronted with their sinfulness. The implicit message to them is that they are all right with God since they came to church on Sunday. That may or may not be the case. Simply going to church is not the criterion by which we are made right with God. I believe that a godly person will go to church, but doing so does not make one godly. I think it is also very important for churches to make sure that what they do in worship is really what it is all about. Too many churches of today are making everything appeal more to the desire to be entertained than to the desire to worship God in true holiness.

I think we must be careful as to what we are calling worship. Worship was never meant to be "convenient" for us. It was never meant to appeal to our feelings and show us a good time. It was never meant to be so blended with the world's approach to entertainment that it loses its distinctiveness. Worship is not for us. It is for God. He is the one who should be focused upon, not us. He is the one who must be pleased with what happened in the worship time, not us. He is the one to be satisfied, not us. Our focus should be on him and not on whether or not the church service "appealed" to us or made us feel good about ourselves. The measure of true worship is not how many people one could attract to it. The measure of true worship is not how comfortable the world feels with it. In fact the world now feels so comfortable with what many churches are doing in the worship hour that see no real difference in it and some other form of entertainment. The danger lies in the fact that they think this kind of "sanctified, self-fulfilling entertainment" carries with it some redemptive power. It does not, and I often wonder just how God feels about what this self-centered, Yuppie, Baby Boomer generation has done to worship in order to make it fit in with the rest of the scope of their lives.

Our worship should, in some way, and to some degree, mirror the gravity of what took place on the cross. It is because of the cross that we are even able to gather in worship. What took place on the day Jesus was sacrificed was serious business. We would not have the privilege of worship without what took place on the cross. It should always be in sight as we worship, and if it is then I think people should think twice before they allow such a low bar to be set for it that the world has no trouble stepping right in and never feeling confronted with the seriousness of the moment.

Chapter 15

Casual Christianity or the Perfect Storm

In the early nineties, a movement was born in the Evangelical world which has grown beyond the expectations of even those who started it. A pastor in Chicago, Bill Hybels, is credited with being the genesis of the contemporary movement and even he has acknowledged the destructive side of it and has stated so. When I concluded my first eight year term on the Executive Committee of the Southern Baptist Convention (SBC), I delivered a short devotional to the subcommittee on which I was serving. In that devotional, I stated that there were two things which were going to have to be confronted and solved in the coming years and that they both begin with a "C." The two things to which I was referring are contemporary worship and Calvinism.

Concerning the contemporary worship style, I made the following observation: There is the risk of losing our denominational identity because people, by their nature, would always be looking for something new and fresh and that they would ultimately seek things which have, traditionally, been outside of who we are as Southern Baptists. I stated that we would finally become confused as to whom we are and if we become confused about it, the society around us will see nothing distinctive about us at all. The result will be that we will blend into the surrounding spiritual landscape to the point that we will no longer be recognized as the Southern

Baptist Convention we have known. This is in the process of happening to us, and it is happening at warp speed.

The second thing I mentioned beginning with a "C" was Calvinism. In the SBC of the early nineties hardly anyone could see that, ultimately, this would be a problem. We have always had Calvinists in our midst, and we have coexisted with no problems. Even a cursory reading of history will show one that, while seventeenth and eighteenth century preachers in our developing country disagreed on this issue, they respected each other, and worked together. After the formation of the SBC in 1845 we might have disagreed with each other but we never sought to bring the SBC to a unified position on the issue. Everyone could believe as he preferred as long as salvation through the blood of Jesus was the unifying factor.

However, I believed then, in 1994, and I believe now, that the Calvinists had an agenda to identify the SBC as a "reformed" convention. While no one denies that many of our prominent founders were Calvinists, there were others who were not. Whatever the case, the SBC began to turn away from that position near the middle of the nineteenth century. This has resulted in those holding to Calvinism being in a small minority among our people and churches. While Calvinism is in the minority in the SBC, it enjoys influence far beyond its numbers. As certain leaders have committed themselves to the "reformed" position for the SBC, they have affected this effort by intentionally raising up an "army" of Calvinists through the educational system that the people of the SBC have paid for with their Cooperative Program dollars. This army is dedicated to the task of seeing that Calvinism is the major theological position of the Southern Baptist Convention. These leaders have known that the young people who have been indoctrinated with the five point Calvinistic model will be just as dedicated to seeing it succeed as those of us were who fought the Battle for the Bible and dedicated ourselves to the task of dealing with the issue of inerrancy.

As I have said on other occasions, I feel it is necessary to reiterate it here: I have no problem with one holding the "reformed" or

Calvinistic theological stance. They are free to believe as they wish, and though I believe they are wrong, I have never let this disagreement hinder my fellowship with those people. Let it also be stated that I do not seek to "convert" a person to my viewpoint. Many lively discussions have been held, but that was the end of it when the discussion was finished. The fact that I have had noted Calvinists lead revivals in my church is proof of the fact that I harbor no ill feelings toward someone who follows that theological model. However, I am opposed to the effort to "reform" the SBC especially through a planned, orchestrated process which has that end as its goal. Anyone who has followed the situation closely knows that one of our theological seminaries in particular is leading the way with this agenda. A second seminary has joined the effort in recent years after employing a new president who is in the process of taking that school into the same camp. That Calvinism was taught at our seminaries in the past was not a big deal to most Southern Baptists, but to intentionally transform those schools for the intended purpose of installing Calvinism in the SBC in order to tout us as a "reformed" convention is too much for me to tolerate. I also sense from my conversations with numerous people all over the convention, that the majority of the people in the SBC share the same feelings. The above statements will be vigorously denied, but as my Grandmother used to say, "The proof is in the pudding."

Back to the contemporary church, competition for members between churches in a given geographical area has resulted in those churches taking the contemporary movement to the extreme in order to attract the largest crowd. When one church goes to a certain level of the contemporary, casual model, others feel they must do the same things or either invent some new twist which will attract more people than their "competition." One noted pastor said that he wanted his music to get more "edgy" because he was tired of losing members to another certain church in town. This approach is dangerous because of the nature of human beings. When people are being entertained, they always want something more sensational than they had the time before. Human nature is never satisfied with its experience and is always seeking something new in order to keep itself entertained. Just ask Disney about this. Why are they always adding new attractions? Once people have been there, done that and have the tee shirt, they want something new in order for the entertainment factor to always be there. Churches are experiencing the same thing.

First, there was the addition of screens with graphics for an audience which was raised on television and video games. Then there was the abandonment of hymn books and those old, musty hymns for the new, bright, entertaining choruses. Of course, they were tailor made for the video screen and for quick and easy access. Besides, one no longer had to hold the hymn book....that heavy old thing. Along with that came the idea that everyone, no matter their physical condition, should stand for thirty minutes or so while they look at the video screen, read the words and sing the choruses. This has its roots in the rock concert scene where young people stand for hours and listen to a rock band. So let's copy that behavior in our church. Surely, it will work here too.

Then, lo and behold, in order to further emulate what the world does, let's bring more entertainment and excitement by adding strobe lights and smoke framed up in a black background. Don't forget to make it so loud that one can hardly stand the decibel levels. That is what one gets with the secular rock bands. I believe this: *the medium becomes the message if one cannot understand the words*. And, in most cases, a person would be hard pressed to understand the words as performed by the "Christian rock bands" which copy the style of the secular bands.

While we are doing all of this, we must do away with that old choir. Too many older people are in it and the young people won't come to our church if they see that. We can replace it with about six people with microphones and a pied piper in order to lead our people in the choruses they are going to read off the screen. This writer is not trying to be sarcastic but when the truth sounds sarcastic, so be it.

This casual approach is also affecting the preachers and staff members. Many preachers and musicians stand before their church each Sunday dressed in a way that my school teachers would not have tolerated and would have sent me home to change. My mother used to make me get new jeans if a hole came in the knee. "Boy, you can't wear those jeans to school, they look terrible," she would say. But, the casual, contemporary philosophy is that one cannot "reach" the people unless they are like them. Quite frankly, from what I have witnessed, those church leaders who hold that philosophy are insulting their members. Are they saying that they dress sloppily because their church members dress the same way? Sounds like it to me.

The people of the world are looking for an example to follow, not someone else like them. Most unsaved sinners are sick of who and what they are and they are looking for something different, something to change their lives both spiritually and socially. But they are made comfortable with whom and what they are when they see pastors, staff and church people who don't seem to be concerned with what they are projecting. I am weary of being expected to condone the idea that the casual, contemporary model is setting the right example and is acceptable. What does the lost person who is looking for answers to life's deepest questions think when he sees a preacher on the platform looking like he just washed his dog, put on a sloppy coat, left his long shirt tail hanging below his coat hem and rushed to the church to preach without even combing his hair? When the preacher and staff project the casual approach to Christianity that is what the people will adopt. Everything rises or falls on leadership, and that is why a leader must make sure that he does not project the wrong thing. The way people dress to attend church these days is downright dishonoring to God. When the pastor bites the bait of casual dress, it results in casual actions which breed a casual approach to God.

Of course, many in the contemporary movement will say, "God is interested in what's on the inside more than He is interested in what's on the outside." Oh, really? Does one mean to say that because God cares about what's on the inside that He does not care about the outside and how we come before Him? If one were called and asked to be in the Oval Office within two days what do you think he or she would do? If he did not have a suit and tie, he would go to the expense of buying one so that he could go into the presence of the President of the United States properly attired. Likewise, a lady would not think of entering the Oval Office in shorts and flip flops. But these same people think it is permissible to come before the God of the universe with an appearance they would never deem appropriate for their president. I tell the people of our church that if a tee shirt and jeans are the best they have, wash them, iron them and wear them to church. That is just fine. But if the best thing one has is a fine tailored suit, then don't wear the tee shirt and jeans. We should come before God in the best we have. How can the pastor be a proper spiritual role model for others unless he sets the right example?

In the Old Testament God was very particular as to how the people constructed the Tabernacle. He outlined it specifically and the people followed his instructions. When it came time to give the instructions on how the Priest should be clothed, God designed the wardrobe very specifically. He told them how the head piece should be made. He designed the breastplate very intricately as well. Certain stones were used for particular reasons known only to God. The robe was of particular significance with the hem to be sewn with red thread. Now, why did God say He wanted red thread? First, the red thread is a "type" of the blood of Christ. Secondly, He said to have the robe hemmed with red thread because that is the way He wanted it, and He does not have to make excuses for anything He says to do. Everything about the design of the Priest's garb was for a purpose. He was to come before the Holy God of the universe in a certain way. He stood out from the crowd. He set the example of how to present oneself before God. The people didn't dress that way but they saw him as an extension of God in their midst.

That is the way preachers should be today. They should stand out as an example and as an extension of God's presence among His people. The same God that prescribed how the Priest was to come before Him is the same God who still sits on the same throne He occupied then. He is the God who does not change in any way, so why do we think that He has now modified His approach as to how we present ourselves to Him? He does not care which century we occupy. He does not care about social implications in today's world. He is unchanging, and I think He still wants us to honor Him by coming before Him in our best attire to signify our awareness of where we are and Who we are coming before.

The ultimate effect of the contemporary, casual approach to Christianity and particularly worship is to lead the people to believe that they really don't have to give up anything or change anything to come before God. They can dress in such a way that they don't have to change clothes in order to go for an afternoon at the lake. One doesn't have to give up their love for rock music, not even for one hour because we are going to give them the same style, volume and appearance while calling it "Christian rock." One doesn't have to be concerned about living the Christian lifestyle because we now tell them that social drinking is just fine according to the Bible. The bar is lowered so low that the world will be glad to come into our church because we will take them as they are and send them on their way as they are with the idea that because they came to church they will go to Heaven when they die. This casual approach leads one to believe that God is happy to take us just as we are with no commitment from us concerning a change in our lives. If the Bible says anything about Christianity it is that we must have a life-changing experience with Jesus Christ.

The contemporary movement combined with Calvinism is, in my opinion, what is causing a decline in baptisms in the SBC. The contemporary movement, in general, does several things which result in the decline in baptisms. First, it does away with the evening worship as an evangelistic event and replaces it with some activities or "educational" opportunities. What they have effectively done is to convert worship time into the old Church Training mode. Question: how many people in the SBC were saved in an evening worship hour? A significant percentage of our people were saved in the evening service. To remove it takes away an opportunity for people to hear the gospel and be saved. Second, it does away with revivals. Not all contemporary churches have ceased to have revivals, but so few do that the effect has been that they are almost nonexistent in those churches. Question: how many people in the SBC were saved during a revival? I can assure the reader that many of them were. To do away with revivals is to limit the number of people who just might give their heart to Jesus. Are the contemporary church leaders saying that an office that is ordained of God, (the evangelist) should not be employed in our churches simply because what he is gifted to do doesn't fit the casual church model any longer and simply won't work in these days? I think this is exactly what is being stated overtly by many and implied by others.

This casual approach to Christianity also tells people that they won't be asked to be dedicated and consistent in their attendance. The casual Christianity approach falsely assumes that people won't come to your church if you demand anything of them. They are not asked to make a public profession of faith as Jesus tells us to do. In the New Testament one could not be a silent or secret Christian. They made the declaration of their faith in Jesus in a public way. Jesus told us to "confess Him before men" and that if we do He will "confess us before the Father," (Matthew 10:32-33). But if we follow the casual model, the idea is that if one has to make a public profession of faith, they will not come to your church. Furthermore, don't place the visitors in any kind of situation in which they will feel uncomfortable in being welcomed. This whole process is a "you do it your way" mentality because we want to make sure that you come to our church even though you will be a "lowest common denominator" Christian and church member. My question is: is the "lowest common denominator Christian" really saved or are they being led astray? This movement is one of the major reasons that the baptisms in the SBC are falling.

Calvinism is contributing to the fall in baptisms as well. I won't take the time to go into the theological reasons I think this is true, but I will point out a simple truth. Calvinism, traditionally, produces few baptisms and smaller churches. This is undeniable and beyond debating. Now, I am sure that one can point to a few Calvinistic churches that are larger than some non-Calvinistic churches, but overall, what I have stated is true. When one weds these two things together, Calvinism and the contemporary church model, the result will be fewer baptisms.

Casual Christianity is the model and mode of the day. This crude society in which we live has influenced even the pulpits of our convention and beyond. More and more, some "preachers" are willing to use crudities in the pulpit. They apparently think it is cute and that it communicates. Here again, if a preacher does such things as using crudities and "light" profanity from the pulpit, he is saying to his audience that they really don't mind him doing that. He feels comfortable doing it and in so doing he insults the sensitivities of many people. The pulpit is no place for cursing or crudities. It is no place to be used to excuse social drinking. It is no place to speak of bodily functions or tell questionable jokes. God is nowhere within a million miles of such a thing. The world has been very effective in convincing the Lord's Church to "let its hair down" and "quit being so stuffy." And, the church has been willing to be convinced if the process will increase the numbers of people who will come. Many of the people who do come into the casual church environment are not coming to be changed. They are coming because the church no longer expects them to change and just because they have come, they feel that when they walk out the door they have done God's bidding and will be welcomed into Heaven when they die. Perhaps these will be in the company of those to whom the Lord says, "Not everyone who says unto Me, 'Lord, Lord,' will enter the Kingdom of Heaven." We are in the Day of Apostasy, I fear.

Chapter 16

The Devastating Effect
of a Postmodern Church

A casual perusal of recent history will reveal that it has not been too many years since the church really made a difference in the way society conducted itself. The public needed a moral compass, and the church was it. When evil and immorality reared its ugly head, the church was the first to confront it and more often than not, was successful in dealing with the problem, thereby protecting the moral and spiritual climate of society. It was the church, along with godly parents, which taught the people what was morally right and socially acceptable. She was viewed as a vital part of the culture while at the same time remaining separate from it to the point that she would be able to influence that culture in a godly fashion. It was the church and godly parents, who had themselves been taught by the church that set the standards for what was good and prudent behavior. She held high the standards of decency which are today being cast aside. People knew it was wrong to "shack up" without being married. They knew that homosexuality was wrong as was profanity and drunkenness. People were warned about the sins of sexual license and pornography. They were told that these things are wrong.

And, when someone stepped over the line and violated what was considered proper spiritually, morally and ethically, the church, as the spiritual Body of Christ who himself must do the forgiving, was the institution of society to which they went for forgiveness. They automatically knew that it was the church which set the standard and that it was to the church that they must go in order to set things right. There is no redemptive power in social, civic or educational organizations, and people knew this. For redemption and peace they automatically turned to the church. It is the church, and only the church, which has the message of redemption, which truly changes lives and saves souls. No other institution or organization has this vital message or the ability to apply it.

In this postmodern era in which we live the situation is quite different, and it will continue to get worse unless the church reclaims some of the high ground it has given up to the world. People now place as much or more confidence in the government and its social programs to provide answers for life as they do the church. In fact, to the average person today, the postmodern church is little more than just another organization present in society. It is a good organization, but to them, it is just that; another social organization which is supposed to make people feel good about who they are.

The true message of the church is too straightforward for people who have absorbed the postmodern frame of thought on how life should be lived. They will not tolerate the actual message of Scripture because they have been taught that it is too narrow and demanding. Not only is it demanding they also feel that it is demeaning. It violates their right to be the person they want to be as prescribed by the politically correct, postmodern culture in which we now live. The devastating thing is that the church has largely accepted this diminished role in society as the proper one for it to fulfill in these days.

She has done this for several reasons. First, it is simply easier to fit in and let society define who the church is and where and how she should conduct herself. It's the "Oh well, I'll just do all I can do under the present circumstances, and I can do no more." This frame of mind simply rewards the lazy and uncommitted. In their minds it exonerates them from the call to make a difference. Churches like this have simply given up while at the same time trying to appear holy. Somehow I do not think that this is what Jesus had in mind when He said, "I will build my church and the gates of hell shall not prevail against it."

Secondly, the church in the postmodern world is being intimidated into subjection. It seems that the only people who do not have complete freedom of speech today are the preachers and the church at large. For fear of losing their tax-exempt status, many men of God have capitulated to the postmodern god called the federal government. I don't find that behavior in Scripture. Suppose Elijah or Daniel or Jeremiah had taken that viewpoint? Can you just hear them saying to God; "Well, you must understand God, the king won't put up with that." So, the church today is timid about the crucial things to which it should speak with boldness. She is religiously fulfilling a perfunctory role in society while becoming weaker and weaker all the time.

Where are the men and the churches who will stand up and say with Bible in hand, "Thus saith the Lord God." If ever a society needed a church to lead it spiritually, morally and ethically this one does, and the church, led my men who are afraid of their shadows, is not filling he bill. When did the ACLU become stronger than the church? I'll tell you when; it was when the church forgot to place its trust in God and His Word to the point that she is intimidated into subjection. It has happened only when God's people allowed it to happen. The world does not mind what the church does as long as she does it within the walls of the sanctuary on Sunday. They just don't want us to bring it outside the sanctuary walls and impact society. That's when they get excited and begin to blow and hiss about how wrong it is for the church to force its opinions on others. "Just stay in the sanctuary and we will tolerate you, but if you come outside then we will violently oppose you." We must regain our boldness and stand up for our Christian faith, or we will slowly lose it by degrees which, incidentally is already happening. We no longer live in an environment which is basically accepting of Christianity, and it will finally eliminate us altogether unless God's people once again become bold and claim the high moral and spiritual ground granted to us by the Lord Jesus himself. Thirdly, the church has become powerless in this age because she desires to become like the society in order to be pleasing to it. The approach which pleases the world and tickles its fancy is totally opposite to what Jesus said the situation should be. He said we were going out as lambs among the wolves. The only way a lamb ever satisfied a wolf was to become its meal, and the world, the flesh and the devil would love to devour us. The marketing of the church is not biblical. Jesus said, "I will build my church." What we must do is to be faithful in proclaiming the gospel and witnessing to the lost as well as ministering to the saints. Then, we must depend on the Lord to add to the church. This whole marketing concept cannot be found in the Bible, and I don't think it pleases God one bit. The world will love and attend a church which poses very little or no challenge to its way of life. These people are led to believe that if they simply attend church they will be acceptable to God. If when they leave the church building they feel good about what they have done, then God must certainly be pleased with it. Their whole concept of worship is that if it makes them feel good and complete, that it was obviously the kind of worship God desires and that it will bring his blessings and exoneration from sin.

This is the postmodern, pragmatic frame of mind which says that if the desired result is achieved, then the process must have been acceptable. Nothing could be further from the truth. When the bar is lowered enough, then the world will find no difficulty in stepping over the bar and attending a particular church. They will not be challenged by anything which is said or done. Yes, the world will flock to such a church, but when they do, then that is exactly what that church has; a church full of the world. This writer still believes that what we do in our worship must, to some degree, mirror the gravity of what took place on the cross. The reason for this is that without the cross we have no reason to be in worship at all. Jesus did not say, "It is finished, now go and have yourselves a good time." To the degree that a church or denomination modifies itself in order to be acceptable to the world, they will cease to have the power to make a difference in the lives of the people in society. If we look, sound and act similarly to the way the world acts, then what testimony do we have, and what advice can we give to them?

We have become, and are in the process of becoming just another organization as the world views them. The supernatural nature of the church is being stripped, away and we are letting it happen and yes, even abetting it. The question must be asked: If we continue to go in the direction we have charted over the past ten or twelve years, what will our children and grandchildren think of the church in the coming years and, more importantly, how much will they value its message? As Paul says in Romans 13: 8-14, we must do two things. We must *wake up*, and we must *change clothes*. We have no business looking and acting and sounding like the world. The contemporary movement which is now so in vogue must remember something. The word "contemporary" literally means "temporary," and that is exactly what Satan wants us to be temporary. This movement is flighty, shallow and appeals to the whims of worldly people who have lost the vision of what the church is or what she is supposed to be. They are there for themselves and not for God, and we must remember that our worship is for God and not for us. He is the one who should be the focus of all we do in worship and not our own gratification. They are the ones who demand to be pleased or they will go somewhere else. They are consumers, not contributors and the church cannot be built on such a foundation.

This contemporary movement is nothing more than the result of people marketing the church, manipulating the environment and appealing to a shallow generation in order to build numbers and prestige. It creates a church with a split personality as the new, contemporary crowd slowly tries to take the direction of the church away from the solid people who founded it. More than one church has experienced this problem and the resulting split. There is much more that could, and indeed, should be said about all of this, but I think that by now the point is well taken. Many people will not totally agree with me on my assessment of the situation, but I have arrived at where I am by carefully examining what is happening in today's church and comparing that with what the Bible says about who and what we are. I will stick by my conclusions. I think that history will prove I am right.

Chapter 17

Three in One

Over the last number of years there have been a number of changes which are causing some confusion in Southern Baptist ranks. Those changes, if incorporated into our Southern Baptist Zion will make us look and act more like Presbyterians than Baptists. I will not attempt to define what all those changes are, but I do want to focus on one in particular. I have observed that many Baptist churches which try to institute the office of elder in their Baptist way of church life find themselves suddenly embroiled in controversy. This does not happen every time, but the problem arises frequently because good Baptist people realize that having the office of elder in their church is something outside the normal practice of our Baptist heritage.

It appears to me that the more the Calvinistic theological model is employed, the more an involved pastor will want to bring the elder system of church governance into the church. Confused by this action, many people resist, asking why this is being done. Others know so little doctrine that they fail to perceive the new direction which is quite different from the traditional one. Many times churches placed in this situation either split or go through a lengthy internal struggle, an unnecessary struggle in my view. The problem may be stated succinctly: the manner in which the "office" of elder is being employed in the new model is not biblical. Consequently, when a pastor imposes on his church the office of elder as an additional office to the pastor and deacons, he is asking his church to adopt an office which the Bible knows nothing about.

Consider: *in the New Testament Church there are only two offices mentioned--pastor and deacon.* One has to strain at a gnat and swallow a camel in order to force the office of elder into the system. First Peter 5:1-6 remains a very important passage which offers clarity to our understanding of biblical church governance. Three words are indicative of the clarity we assert: "elder" (v.1),"feed" (v.2), and "taking the oversight" (v.2). All three of these terms refer to the same person, the person serving as pastor of the church. The term "elder"(v.1) is "presbuteros" in the Greek language. One can easily see the resemblance between that word and the word "Presbyterian." It is translated "elder" and refers to the pastor serving as spiritual statesman of the church. In other words, the pastor is the one who sets the theological agenda for the church. He is the one to whom the people to get spiritual guidance. The pastor sets the tone for the spiritual depth of the church. He is the elder; but he is not a separate person from the pastor. Elder and pastor are one and the same. Hence, the pastor is one and the same.

In verse two, we find the word, "feed." The word translated "feed" is "poimen" and refers to the spiritual leader, the pastor. In addition, the verb form of the word translated "feed" is "poimaino;" it refers to one who rules and acts as shepherd. That is, the pastor tends the flock. He takes care of them and guides them. The problems of the church are brought to him. The sick depend on him. The instruction which properly guides the church is given by the pastor. He "feeds" the flock by preaching to them and instructing them in God's Word.

In fact, preaching is his *main* task. Therefore, a church which has a pastor who spends the proper time preparing to preach God's Word is a fortunate church indeed. Sadly, this portion of the pastor's duties is usually the one on which he spends the least time.

One of our greatest problems today is that our Baptist people don't know what they believe or why they believe what they believe. Too frequently, the fault for this resides squarely in the lap of the preachers. While the pastor can't make his congregation absorb what he preaches, neither can he expect them to be correct in doctrine unless he feeds them the Word.

So, the pastor is both the elder statesman (v.1) and the shepherd (v.2). Furthermore, we find the phrase "taking the oversight" relevant to a biblical understanding of "elder" as well (v.2). The phrase "taking the oversight" is one word in the Greek, "episkopos," and means "overseer." Sounding similar to "Episcopal," it is the word from which we get the term "Bishop." Therefore, it refers to the pastor as overseer or administrator of the church, managing the affairs of the church. Any church which is run by a committee will have problems because the biblical approach is for the pastor to be the one overseeing the church. The point is not that committees are unnecessary. Indeed we could not run the church without committees to take care of various functions. Rather, the point is, committees must come under the supervision of the Pastor who serves as the overseer of the church; that is, he is the Bishop of the church.

In verse one, Peter says "The elders which are among you I exhort." He then goes on in to give them the exhortation and instruction concerning the function of elders. He says "lead your people spiritually; preach to them; feed them God's Word; guide them properly..." (Harrell paraphrase). Moreover, he tells them "take charge; manage the situation; oversee the church." So it is easy to see that Peter was not offering instruction about three people in multiple *roles* but one person in multiple *functions*--the pastor. Those who institute the office of "elder" in the church are forming a new office the Bible does not institute itself. Biblically, the only two offices in the church are the pastor and the deacon.

Consider the Apostle Paul's instructions to Timothy (3:1-10). In referring to the pastor (vv.1-6), Paul points to the administrative portion of the pastor's task when he refers to him as "bishop" (v.1). Later, Paul says that the deacon must qualify for his position just as the pastor does (v.8).

Notice the Apostle Paul mentions only two offices: *bishop* (administrator, manager, pastor and elder statesman) and *deacon*. The deacons neither run the church nor are given the task of setting church agenda. That is the job of the bishop (administrator; manager). Instead, the deacon is a servant (diakanos). Deacons assist the pastor in serving the church's needs. Hence, deacons biblically constitute the second office in the church.

Paul also deals with the same subject in Titus (1:5-9). Paul tells Titus to "ordain elders in every city as I had appointed thee" (v.5). Afterward, he lays down the pastoral qualifications (v.6) and then says "For a bishop must be blameless..." (v.7). It remains obvious by his wording that the "elder" (v.5) is also the "bishop" (v.7).

Baptists are, as every Baptist ought to know, a congregational people. They don't have a hierarchy over them to govern them as many other denominations do. Every pastor should be a "pastor-teacher." That term is used by Paul in Ephesians 4:11 where the Apostle is talking about the gifts given to the church. A.T. Robertson observes that Paul lumped the two designations together. The two words should be hyphenated designating that it is actually one individual. Thus, the Pastor *feeds* the flock, *rules* the flock, *guides* the flock, and, according to what Paul says to Timothy, *teaches* the flock.

Finally, we do well to remember when Baptists institute a model for church polity which includes the office of elder in addition to the pastor and deacons, they are actually violating the Baptist Faith and Message which serves as our doctrinal guide as Southern Baptists. The Baptist Faith and Message recognizes only two offices in congregational polity, pastor and deacon. While we are not a creedal people, and therefore have no ultimate authority but the Bible, we nonetheless have a confession which clearly demonstrates our theological heritage. And, our confession states, as does the New Testament, we historically have only two church offices, neither of which is the "elder" in its extra-biblical sense.

One may see how the terms "teaching elder" and "ruling elder" are confusing if they refer to someone other than the pastor. It seems to me that they are actually calling an assistant to the pastor an "elder." If that is what some are referencing, then they are wrong again because those staff members performing certain tasks are not the elder but an assistant to the pastor. "Associate to the pastor" either in education or administration is more correct and less confusing than either "teaching elder" or "ruling elder." I'm sure some of those in favor of instituting the elder approach in Baptist churches will say that I just simply don't understand. But what I actually don't understand is why people, primarily our Calvinist friends, want to force Baptist churches into an "elder model" which surely resembles the Presbyterian tradition more than the Baptist. In summary, when one goes beyond the two biblical offices or pastor and deacon, he or she structures the church in a way which goes beyond the biblical model. Consequently, Christian harmony will not be produced. Unfortunately, as stated earlier, some seem so wed to an agenda to promote Calvinism in our Baptist churches that they simply won't recognize that the Bible does not authorize the separate office of elder. Even so, a church properly constructed will have a Pastor (elder, shepherd or ruler, and the administrator), and the office of Deacon who are servants of the church, assisting the Pastor in certain duties.

This writer thinks that if one wants to take Baptist churches into a system which has the elder as a separate office in addition to the Pastor and deacon, then they should simply either form themselves into a Presbyterian type congregation or else join one. Leave the Baptists alone. We do not want nor do we need to copy the Presbyterians in church form or in their theology. Identify with them, but don't ask Baptists to modify themselves in order to satisfy the Calvinistic leanings to which some in our convention are now firmly joined.

Chapter 18

Godly or Cool?

For the generation which is getting a little older it is quite disconcerting and puzzling to observe that it is now more popular to be cool than it is to be Godly. Only a few short years ago, Pastors were men who stood out from the crowd because of the example they set in an effort to lead people into a Godly, committed way of life. They looked different from the crowd because they set an example in their dress and in their good conduct. Men of God honored their position by dressing in a professional manner which was neat and orderly. It helped people understand that here was someone from which they could take an example as to how to conduct themselves as a Christian. These same men were not only identified by their dress, they were respected because of the way in which they conducted themselves in and out of the pulpit. People looking for hope and help looked to the Pastor for a heavenly example. These men were more than mere men. They represented God to those around them.

In those days, what one believed was the most important thing. How could a Pastor impart proper understanding of the scripture unless he believed and revered it himself? He was concerned more with being right than he was with being "cool." In fact, being cool was something which was a million miles from his conception of what a Pastor and preacher was supposed to be. It never entered his mind to be "cool." It simply was not part of the mix. These men from yesteryear, were disciplined and committed to being sure they led the people properly and set the proper example. It never crossed their minds that they needed to identify with the people by being like them even to the lowest common denominator of acceptability. The Pastor was supposed to set an example of what we should strive to be like. He never dreamed that he would be expected to downgrade himself in order to win their affection or attention. Where was the example in that?

But, today there are many young preachers who feel that it is a necessity to be "cool" in order to be accepted and build a big church. The idea is that descending to the least common denominator of dress and example will enable people to see that you are a "regular, cool guy" who can identify with them. In other words, being "cool" is the identifying mark of today. People just love it. But, we are supposed to elevate people, not fall to whatever level makes them comfortable.

The Pastor or preacher should identify with his people. But, his identity with them should be grounded in the fact that they identify with him because they have been elevated to his Godly standard instead of his becoming like the masses in order to find an identity with them.

In previous generations, what a man believed as well as his conduct and example was what was important. He elevated his people with his preaching, teaching, conduct and example. But, today, "cool" can say or do just about anything because it sounds cool and confirms that they are just that....cool. When one says or demonstrates that he wants to be "cool" he is actually saying that he wants to be acceptable. He doesn't want to stand out from the crowd. "Why, they will leave if they are confronted by anything which says they should be living or believing differently, he will say." The fact that a man is a great Bible scholar-expositor remains secondary to whether or not he is acceptable to the populace. Being popular and "with it" (cool) is a necessity for success especially if one wants to be in the "in crowd." Being "cool" is a human effort to go places and achieve things that might not be on God's agenda for a person.

But, one will say; "When I get them here because they are not threatened by me, then I can preach the gospel to them." Sorry. It won't work. The message is lost in the environment. The crowd that will be drawn won't really want to hear the message and apply it. They just want to go to heaven and they think that if they are in church and really feel good about their experience then that is the ticket. The "punch" of the message is lost because someone who looks and, in many cases talks and acts just like them, is delivering it and his example is no better than theirs.

It's "cool" to be edgy. Some try to see what they can get away with. Just how far can I go, they will think. Because they are the preacher and have the authority of that position behind them they think the people will not challenge them or be offended by off color language, remarks or insinuations. After all, he is the authority. The sad thing is that people will put up with such actions. They have slowly been programmed to feel that there is nothing wrong with the environment or the content. Certainly, there is nothing wrong with the preacher. He can say those things and imply those things because he is God's man and that should not be questioned. Besides he is the coolest of the cool. Everyone is talking about him so that makes him successful and, by implication, makes him right in whatever he says and does. "I like him. He makes me feel good about me and that makes him acceptable and cool."

The great Pastors and preachers of yesterday and today are not known as "cool." They are looked upon and respected because of the godly example they set and not because they fit the desirable mold of today's mindset. What we have today in many cases is a "spiritual entertainer" who relies more on methods to excite and entertain than on what he should be telling them. A desire to return and see the next show is greater than the desire to hear a word from God. Human nature always demands more than was done the last time or they will get bored with what is happening. That is why some preachers today are continually trying to find ways to make the next gathering more "electric" than the last. It's "cool" to be edgy and groovy. It meets the demand of a "video clip" and "sound byte" generation who really wants no more than that.

We are tolerating things in our churches that are embarrassing to Godly people who believe the Bible. Things which are said and taught are things which even the world did in a dark corner a few years ago. But, just because the church is allowing such things to take place in its midst does not make it Godly or Biblical. Our Godly preaching forefathers would "turn over in their graves" if they heard some of the language being used in church today. They would be absolutely horrified to hear young preachers telling people it is acceptable to drink alcohol. They would be even more horrified to hear someone talk of sex in the way it is being discussed today. How far we have drifted! And it is all in the name of the "cool" and acceptable.

Each succeeding generation can only learn from the examples set by the previous generation. They will also "fill in the blanks" with their own accepted moral and spiritual mores when proper guidance was either not taught or not learned. It is incumbent upon each generation to make sure that they set the right example so that their offspring will be pointed in the right direction. They in turn will pass along to the their generation only so much as they have learned. The result is usually that the next generation will "fill in some blanks" as they seek to meet the expectations of the evolving society. Therein is the downgrade. If we continue down the road which many are choosing today, what will the next generation look like? Then what will their offspring consider normal activity?

I realize that anyone who is a part of the "cool" generational movement will find much to criticize about this little article but there are many others who will see great value in it. It cannot be denied that in the past twenty years we have flirted with many things that our forefathers would never have imagined. And, in the process we are losing our unique identity as people who set a Godly standard for others to follow. We are in the process of becoming just another denomination in a vast sea of denominations. If we keep going in the direction we are now headed, we will, one day, be heaped in with all the other denominations which have compromised away their witness and who have lost their ability to influence the world with great spiritual power and authority.

Chapter 19

Living in a Spiritual Vacuum

We live in what is probably the most "spiritual" age since man was placed on the earth. It was predicted in the late eighties that the decade of the 90's and leading up to the 21st century would be a time of great spiritual revival and this has proven to be true. But, there is only one problem. This revival of spirituality has not and is not necessarily a revival of Christian spirituality.

The worldly brand of spirituality involves many things: séances …communicating with the dead or what is known as necromancy. There is the Wiccan religion or witchcraft. It involves the worship of nature, casting of spells, magic, fortune telling and related activities. The New Age religion which embraces reincarnation, crystals, pagan deities and many other facets of spiritual interest is perfectly suited for a self-centered generation which wants to craft its own religion. These are only a few mentioned to make the point that spiritual activity is not always Christian activity and should not be confused as such.

The spirituality of the world is further evidenced by people who confess Christianity but who blend different beliefs together in order to come to a personal conclusion concerning their individual belief system. It is as if a person can develop his own system and by remaining faithful to it, he has somehow satisfied God and is right with Him. Many Christians blend certain aspects of several world religions together with a grain of Christianity and think they are Christians. They have a "spiritual system" and by having such a thing, they feel that God should be satisfied with them simply because they are happy with themselves. In blending other "spiritual" thought with Christianity, people are trying to "cover all the bases" never realizing that Christianity blended with anything else is no longer Christianity. So, in an effort to "cover all the bases", they really cause themselves to "foul out."

To the modern secular mind there is even such a thing as being spiritual without being religious. A recent survey of college students found that while 45% of them claimed to be Christian, a full 35% said they were "spiritual" but not "religious." The question is: how can one be spiritual without being religious? Apparently in this current environment it is very easy to so class one's self.

What we need today is a genuine revival of true Christian spirituality. God has always worked through revival in orders to stir and change His People. True revival will lead us and enable us to see ourselves as we really are and then it leads people to submit to God and allow Him to change them into what He wants them to be. Genuine revival can only take place when we can truly access ourselves, confess our sins and turn our hearts toward God. There is a great spiritual vacuum in the lives of people that can only be answered with a vital relationship with God. Most people are aware of the spiritual emptiness of their souls and they desire something to fill that void. The message of the Bible is so very important because it tells us how to have that void filled and it tells us God's method of filling it: Salvation through His Son, Jesus Christ. There is no other way. Man has looked for another way for thousands of years and he is still just as frustrated as ever when he tries to do it on his own. If another way could be found, I think man would have found it by now. That is what all this worldly "spirituality" is really all about: trying to find a way to fill the void without using God's plan which is faith in Jesus Christ. Remember this...being spiritual is not the same as being saved and being in a right relationship with God through His Son, Jesus Christ.

The end result of all this is that people find themselves even more frustrated as they try to make some sense out of the spiritual vacuum in which they are living. The vacuum is not going to be filled by climbing a high mountain to find a holy man who will tell you the secrets of life. The spiritual vacuum will be filled as close to you as your own heart when you trust in Christ for salvation and commit your life to Him.

CPSIA information can be obtained at www.ICGtesting.com
Printed in the USA
LVOW090346100812

293673LV00003B/3/P